DESIGN THAT SCALES

CREATING A SUSTAINABLE DESIGN SYSTEM PRACTICE

T0091871

Design That Scales

Creating a Sustainable Design System Practice

By Dan Mall

Rosenfeld Media, LLC

125 Maiden Lane

New York, New York 10038

USA

On the Web: www.rosenfeldmedia.com

Please send errata to: errata@rosenfeldmedia.com

Publisher: Louis Rosenfeld

Managing Editor: Marta Justak

Interior Layout: Danielle Foster

Cover Design: Heads of State

Illustrator: Pooja Jadav

Indexer: Marilyn Augst

Proofreader: Sue Boshers

ISBN: 1- 959029-21-5

ISBN 13: 978-1-959029-21-2

LCCN: 2023945866

Printed and bound in the United States of America

For everyone who's built a career
designing forms and tables and cards
and doesn't know what's next.

Who Should Read This Book?

If you're a designer, engineer, or product manager at an enterprise that thinks there are more efficient ways to work at scale, this book is for you. If you're a lead or an executive who can effect change but are unsure exactly what change to effect, this book is for you. If you think digital product work can be more collaborative, this book is for you. If you think work can be more fun if you could somehow eliminate the boring stuff, this book is for you.

This is a book about process. It's about the counterintuitive process of creating design systems in a way that makes it easier to get traction and investment. It's about the new process that designers, engineers, product managers can adopt with a design system at their disposal. It's about the worthy process of getting teams to contribute to your design system so that it gets better for everyone. It's ultimately about connecting your design system directly to the crucial process that creates value for your organization's customers, users, and constituents.

Design systems can do all of that, if you know how. This book contains concepts and theory that give design systems context, as well as examples of how you can practice design systems successfully and stories for how others have done it too. This book will help you think about design systems in a different way than you may have before.

Even though there's a chapter called "Design System Fundamentals," this isn't a "nuts and bolts" book. You'll only find a handful of definitions and foundational discussions here, as many other people and texts have previously covered that in great detail. This book isn't a "how-to" book. Even though there are code examples, this book isn't a collection of design system tutorials. This book spends most of its pages on the guidance and relationships needed to create, use, and maintain design systems successfully at large organizations.

What's in This Book?

Chapter 1: "Why Design Systems" makes the case for why a design system is a worthwhile undertaking for most organizations managing two or more digital products.

Many teams don't know the difference between design systems, component libraries, and UI kits. **Chapter 2:** "Design System Fundamentals" lays out some important distinctions about why design systems are so tricky to define.

Chapter 3: "The Parts of a Design System Product" breaks down the ecosystem around a design system to understand the context in which a design system must succeed.

Chapter 4: "The Broken Business of Buy-In" deconstructs the standard wisdom of how design systems are sold to understand why it almost never works—and what's a better way instead.

Chapter 5: "Pilots—The Best Way to Start and Sustain a Design System" walks through a counterintuitive process for successfully creating a new design system that proposes a low-friction path to automatic contribution.

Chapter 6: "Governance and Contribution" goes over the who, what, where, when, and why of design systems to establish a simple, repeatable process.

Chapter 7: "Roles and Responsibilities" and **Chapter 8:** "Process and Workflow for Design Systems" discuss the people involved in connected design system work, where they fit, and useful workflows for how they can best collaborate.

Chapter 9: "Success Metrics for a Design System" covers both general and organization-specific metrics of success for design systems to hit.

Chapter 10: "Evangelism Never Stops" discusses the oft-neglected task of marketing a design system to the people who need to use it: internal designers, engineers, and product managers.

The **Conclusion** rounds out the book by reminding us why any of this design system stuff matters in the first place.

What Comes with This Book?

This book's companion website (**rosenfeldmedia.com/books/design-that-scales**) contains a blog and additional content. The book's diagrams and other illustrations are available under a Creative Commons license (when possible) for you to download and include in your own presentations. You can find these on Flickr at **www.flickr.com/photos/rosenfeldmedia/sets/**.

FREQUENTLY ASKED QUESTIONS

What is a design system?

A design system can be many things: a visual language, a library of code snippets, a collection of artboards in a design tool, a way of doing design, and much more. In this book, I talk primarily about design systems as an organizational practice. **Chapter 2**, "Design System Fundamentals," explores each of these kinds of design systems in more detail.

Why are design systems important?

About five billion people use the internet each day, and the average person spends over six hours online daily. Designing websites, apps, and digital content at scale is imperative for keeping up with the ever-increasing demand for information and services online. Understanding design systems and how to work with them is already a job prerequisite for digital designers, engineers, and product folks at many organizations, and that trend continues to increase.

Aren't design systems just for designers?

Absolutely not! Design systems are exciting because they are one of the few tools that equally serve the proverbial three-legged stool of design, engineering, and product. **Chapter 7**, "Roles and Responsibilities," describes all the roles and responsibilities that can exist on a design system team.

Will this book teach me how to make a design system?

Yes and no. If you're looking for detailed how-to for setting up UI kits in design tools like Figma or prop settings in languages like React or Angular, there are many online articles and courses that do a better job of that. I chose not to cover those kinds of topics in this book because that's not usually where most design systems fail. Most design systems fail because they aren't integrated early enough into the grain of how an organization operates, so this book focuses mostly on how to do just that.

I've made design systems before in just a few days. Does this topic really warrant a whole book?

It's true that a skilled practitioner can create design system artifacts like Figma UI kits and code libraries very quickly. However, a design system practice takes time to establish. It's not that the tasks take long; it's that design systems practices are exercises in cultural change, and change takes time to permeate through an organization in a way that sticks. **Chapter 6**, "Governance and Contribution," explains the who, what, where, when, and why design systems take time—time that's well spent.

Will this book recommend tools that make design system work easier?

It's an exciting time in design system tooling because new applications, plug-ins, and software are coming out every day! While there are a handful of tools mentioned throughout the book, the tools are too new and change too often for me to call out any as having stood the test of time.

CONTENTS

FOREWORD

When you hear the name Susan Kare, you think of icons. When you hear the name John Maeda, the intersection of design and technology comes to mind. And most importantly, when you hear the name Dan Mall, you think of design systems.

Congratulations! If you are reading this foreword, it means that you have just bought a book that is not only going to help you, but also the people around you. If you are simply browsing this book and wondering "Should I buy this book?" I'm here to tell you that the answer is "YES! Absolutely YES!"

Dan Mall is fundamentally the most experienced person on the planet to talk about design systems. His experience reaches far and wide, and this book is going to give you all the tools you need to create and maintain a design system. Not just a design system that will work right now, but a sustainable design system. One that designers, engineers, and others will thank you for building for years to come.

This book will help you flip the apprehensive mindset that design systems are used to stifle innovation into a mindset that shows designers and engineers they have more freedom than ever.

I met Dan several years back at a design conference. We were sitting next to each other at a dinner we were both attending, and the two of us "nerded" out for quite some time about the role of design operations and design systems on design teams. Everything we were talking about made sense. We just needed to tell the world how to leverage these skill sets. We wanted to make happier and more successful teams. This is your chance to hear from the maestro himself.

Now stop reading my foreword and let's get reading.

—Meredith Black
Founder, DesignOps Assembly

Design Systems: An Advantage for Designing at Scale

I'm fortunate to have worked and consulted with people at hundreds of organizations on their design systems. Most of them do it wrong.

The story usually goes like this.

After spending weeks, months, and even years designing and building the same interface elements over and over, a small faction gets wise and decides that creating a handful of reusable, common solutions will help everyone get out of the grind of reinventing the wheel every time. They design and code interface building blocks like form elements, tables, headers, footers, buttons...the elements they think everyone uses or could use.

They start to use this new library themselves, and it works! They're finishing their work faster, and they're even seeing an added bonus of more consistency across the work.

Not ones to be selfish, they think others would benefit from this new library, too, so they share it with other teams within the company. And then...

Crickets.

They hear nothing back for a while. Once they finally do, the responses are both unexpected and undesirable.

"We tried using it, but there were a few elements missing."

"We weren't really sure how to use it because there wasn't much documentation."

"We don't have time to learn a new library right now."

Discouraged, the team decides that they *could* address these legitimate objections that teams raised, but doing so would take them away from their main work, and they can't afford to do that right now. Their library sits there, lonely and unused.

Unbeknownst to this team, another team elsewhere in the organization just went through the same exercise with the same result. To make things worse, neither of these teams knew that the other team was also working on this, that a few more teams in this organization did the same thing last year, and that others did it the year before that. Only a handful of people who have been with the company for a few years know about all of these false starts.

I call these collections of failed attempts *design system ghost towns* and *design system graveyards*. Almost every organization has them. They're always well-intentioned. Teams do what seems sensible and intuitive, and it rarely works. Why don't they work?

Most teams approach creating a design system as a project first. They're unprepared for the reality that design system adoption is dependent on changing organizational culture—namely, getting everyone to think and work differently than they're used to. Most design system efforts start with a battle against the status quo. Modern digital organizations typically structure teams and work in silos; it's supposedly more efficient that way. Design system work quickly bumps into the edges of those silos, and successful design systems break through them, often prompting reorganization. The naïve designer or engineer, who thought a few simple tools could help everyone quickly, finds themself ill-equipped to address the barrage of concerns that design systems inevitably surface.

Quickly, a *design system as a project* that somehow thrives will evolve into a *design system as a product* by necessity. Like any good product, it needs investment, a dedicated team, a roadmap, marketing, and—most importantly—loyal customers and users.

Teams that run design system products eventually realize that they need more. Design systems are most needed at large enterprises that manage many digital products. Design systems require people with different skills to work together, and that's often unusual and foreign for many organizational cultures. The process of making digital products nowadays needs people who can understand typographic scales, model-view-controller patterns, and customer acquisition costs, all at once. Design systems have the potential to bring it all together, but that means people using design systems need to develop new habits. They need the ability to try new things, experience small wins early, and build momentum that adds up to larger wins over time.

Overall, the most mature kind of design system is a practice.

Just what to practice, though, is often elusive. Done well, design systems are fitting vehicles for efficiency, innovation, and job satisfaction. This book will show you how to create and sustain a thriving design system practice so you can effectively design at scale.

CHAPTER 1

Why Design Systems?

Think about all the Google products you used today. Maybe you checked your email using Gmail during some early part of your day. Perhaps you drove to your office or to an appointment using Google Maps to help with directions. You probably needed more info about something, and you looked it up on Google Search, perhaps using Google Chrome. Maybe you collaborated with a colleague on a Google Doc or Google Sheet. Maybe you watched a video on YouTube. Maybe you did all of that on an Android mobile device.

As a user, you probably didn't give much thought as to what it took on the Google end to make this kind of day possible for you. And you shouldn't! All you should care about is whether or not you're getting the experience you want from using these applications.

Systems Connect Organizations

But what does it take for Google to deliver this holistic experience for you? As of this writing, Google—technically Google's parent company, Alphabet Inc.—employs almost 140,000 people. Google also works with many external partners and agencies to help them accelerate and innovate on the digital products they create for their users. Keeping thousands of people aligned from a design and engineering perspective requires some kind of system, a set of things working together as parts of a mechanism or an interconnecting network. For organizations that make digital products, one of those systems is called a *design system*. Here's my definition:

> A design system is a connected, package-managed, version-controlled software product that contains the smallest set of components and guidelines a particular organization needs to make digital products consistently, efficiently, and happily.

This is a mouthful! I'll explore and explain each of these words and phrases in greater detail in Chapters 2, "Design System Fundamentals," and 9, "Success Metrics for a Design System."

Google's design system is called *Material Design*.[1] In Google's own words, Material Design is "an adaptable system of guidelines, components, and tools that support the best practices of user interface design." (See how close that is to my definition?) Without Material

---

1 "Material Design," Google, **https://m3.material.io/**

Design, Google employees and partners would be left to design and build each product and screen and interaction and element from scratch each time, creating an incredible amount of effort and unwarranted variation. Having a shared system like Material Design means Google designers and engineers can quickly reference common solutions (Figure 1.1) that are ready for implementation.

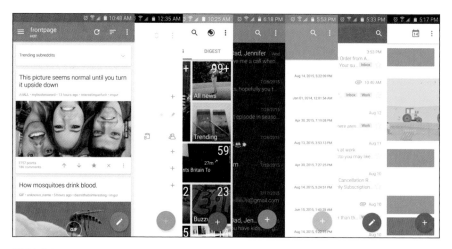

FIGURE 1.1

No matter what Google application you use, the floating action button component always provides easy access to the primary action of a screen in the bottom-right corner.

Design systems aren't just better for the designers, engineers, product managers, and rest of the team creating digital products. Design systems prove better for users, too, because they don't have to relearn interaction conventions from application to application. A 2016 Forrester study[2] found that consistency in customer experience led to a 24% increase in revenue, and design systems tend to create interface consistency by their nature (Figure 1.2).

---

2 Dylan Czarnecki and Harley Manning, "Customer Experience Drives Revenue Growth, 2016," Forrester, June 21, 2016, **www.forrester.com/report/ Customer-Experience-Drives-Revenue-Growth-2016/RES125102**

FIGURE 1.2
Even if you've only used one Google product header, you know how to use them all.

But maybe you don't use Google products.

Maybe you use Microsoft products. Microsoft takes the same approach with their Fluent Design System.[3]

Maybe you use IBM products. IBM takes the same approach with their Carbon Design System.[4]

Maybe you use Salesforce products. Salesforce takes the same approach with their Lightning Design System.[5]

The list goes on and the point is clear: organizations that create and maintain two or more digital products often turn to design systems to help them solve the problem of digital product management at scale. If your organization wants to scale digital products, design systems aren't just a good idea, they're an inevitability.

Common Benefits of Design Systems

Design system aficionados often espouse three main benefits of design systems:

- **Using a design system advocates efficiency.** Starting from scratch and reinventing the wheel each time a digital product is made is a major culprit of digital overspending. Having proven solutions at the ready helps teams address problems more quickly.

- **Using a design system generates consistency.** Design systems prioritize reusability across digital products, and reusability is the main ingredient in consistency.

---

3 "Fluent Design System," Microsoft, **https://fluent2.microsoft.design/**

4 "Carbon Design System," IBM, **https://carbondesignsystem.com/**

5 "Lightning Design System," Salesforce, **www.lightningdesignsystem.com/**

- **Using a design system spawns innovation.** Moving designers and engineers from creating everything from scratch to reusing common interface and interaction remedies frees up their time to address unfamiliar problems and invent solutions for them.

I also like to add a fourth:

- **Using a design system bestows relief.** Digital product teams regularly stress over unrealistic deadlines and wicked problems. Design systems give them a cheat code that gives them time and space back so they can breathe more easily.

Realizing these benefits is easier said than done. Many successful design system initiatives instigate cultural and organizational transformation, and unsuccessful attempts frequently die due to organizational politics. An ingrained and lasting design system practice is necessary to bring about these benefits.

Who Are Design Systems For?

Anyone who works on a digital product team can benefit from a design system. While this book focuses primarily on the roles of the famed "three-legged stool"—design, engineering, and product—design system work includes many other disciplines like content, QA, research, illustration, business analytics, behavioral science…any discipline typically found on a digital product team.

Unsurprisingly, these are also the roles useful in making a design system for an organization. It's natural for a design system to start within a particular discipline like design, IT, or UX. These design systems often fail to gain traction, because it's too easy for the rest of the organization to see it as "someone else's library." A design system needs to belong to everyone, which means it can't really belong to anyone. Working on, contributing to, and maintaining a design system is truly a democratic and collaborative exercise. The rest of this book will show you how to avoid a siloed birth for a design system and instead create one that eventually represents an entire organization.

Questions for Reflection

- Does your team or organization manage two or more digital products?
- What kind of efficiencies in tools and processing could your organization benefit from?
- Do you already have a design system in your organization?

Hayley Hughes is a seasoned design system expert who has worked at some of the largest and well-known enterprise organizations of our time. I asked her a few questions about her experience with design systems and what it takes to succeed in the space.

What is a design system to you?

To me, design systems are a *community of practice* made up of diverse teams within an organization. This practice involves teams collaborating in an ever-evolving feedback loop of observing, making, and reflecting on what a quality experience means for their users, and how to deliver it. The community creates and governs shared platforms and tooling for scaling insights, standards, assets, and services across an enterprise.

You've worked on design systems at the largest scale at some of the world's largest organizations. What skills do you need to work at that level?

At larger organizations, the design system supports thousands of people, from in-house teams to external partners. It needs to work for diverse audiences in a variety of geographies and environments using different devices and technologies. With so many use cases, the system needs to enable unity, not uniformity—rallying teams to create cohesion across experiences, while giving them flexibility and a wide range of expression.

Going from small to large companies is as much a mindset shift as it is a skillset. You stop thinking of systems as a purely pixel-and-code craft and start thinking of systems as a state craft of operationalizing people and practices.

Operational skills like facilitation, coaching, and diplomacy help you organize movements and manage change with large groups of people. That means you drive alignment conversations between a dozen teams. You coordinate rollouts that cascade changes across hundreds of products. You create educational materials for training design system trainers. You build domain knowledge in the product development cycle and identify ways that systems can improve institutional capacity. You look for patterns—matchmaking people and resources. Pixels and code still matter, but you hire others with the skills that it takes to do those jobs, while coaching them on the skills it takes to scale systems.

continues

What are some commonalities between every design system you've worked on?

I've worked on a handful of design systems at IBM, Airbnb, Nike, and Shopify. One reason I chose to work on these systems is because the people leading them have common values. First, they understand that the purpose of design systems is to improve the quality of decision-making on teams versus just shipping faster. Second, they really care about driving collaboration across teams and introducing changes in a thoughtful way. Third, these teams prioritize equitable work in areas like accessibility, inclusion, localization, and ethics.

From a team size perspective, most systems I've worked on had a core team of designers and developers that might range anywhere in size between a handful to a few dozen people at any given time. They've all had a shared design language, component libraries, documentation site, and enablement program for training and partnering with product teams. Usually, the system has been positioned horizontally, reporting in through a design, operations, or infrastructure function.

What are some differences in organizations that make each of their design systems unique from one another?

Every design system I've worked on has been at a different stage of maturity. IBM's design system was built from the ground up, developing a design language for everything—not just the software and hardware, but also the physical buildings, business cards, events, advertisements, you name it. Airbnb had trouble getting people to use the system, so I was asked to help drive adoption. Shopify wanted to expand to become a system of systems. This meant focusing on governance and enabling teams to create local systems. Nike's system needed to become more flexible to support more differentiation across brands, geographies, and use cases. Every system has similar problems, but depending on which stage of maturity they're in, you might be prioritizing one over another.

How did your career path prepare you to work on design systems so effectively?

There is no one career path that leads you to being effective in design systems. I've had teammates who were former biologists that were experts in feedback loops or lawyers who knew how to handle open source licensing. People in design systems come from all different kinds of backgrounds.

A common theme in a design system career path is the idea of being hybrid, or showing interest and capability in multiple domains. This concept most often refers to hybrid skills in design and development, but there are many types of hybrids. Part of becoming a hybrid involves trying on many hats before defining your role in design systems. By doing so, you become an interdisciplinary thinker with more empathy for others.

I wouldn't call myself a hybrid, but I have spent most of my career doing interdisciplinary thinking. I first worked at nonprofits focused on influencing political and environmental systems. Then I worked at restaurants and art museums that created hospitality, brand, and wayfinding systems. In grad school, I studied healthcare and local food systems. Now, I'm focused on design language systems.

What advice would you give to someone looking to break into a design system career?

Look for the holes. If you're able to sell the holes as an actual problem, then you can put yourself in a position to fix them. Do the research to show that you know what teams need. For example, if you're seeing issues with accessibility in a product experience, dig deeper. The business should also care because it probably has requirements it has to meet around compliance to avoid litigation. Combine the user needs and the business requirements into a compelling opportunity, and solve for that.

You don't even need to say the words *design system* at first, even if that's what you're technically making. Once you solve it, you've built trust to ask for more investment, perhaps another teammate or resources to keep filling other "holes." Keep tracking and measuring the outcomes of the problems you're solving. Eventually, these things snowball where you can share full case studies and reveal the system that powers them.

continues

What encouragement would you give to design system veterans?

If you're in an organization that struggles to reward systems work and promote systems people into higher levels, don't give up. There are periods in your career when no matter what you say, people just won't "get" systems. Maybe it's because they require a tolerance for some degree of complexity. There will be other times where you'll have incredible advocates who not only "get" systems but invest in you and your team. There's some peace in knowing that this is an endless cycle, as stakeholders and investors come and go over the years.

What we have control over is the ability to apply the holistic approach we take to solving any type of problem within an organization. Don't just make decisions. Study how decisions get made. People who move into a systems leadership role need to shift their practice toward understanding: How are decisions made, contributed, governed, learned about? Our jobs are to make sure that process, that decision workflow is as seamless and easy to do and conducive to good outcomes as possible. That's system lifecycle work.

Lastly, remember to ask: Where is the most impact you can make inside or even outside your organization with your skills in design systems? Your answer might be about helping people work better together. It might be about training people to be systems thinkers. Maybe it's about bringing together the entire organization and the end-to-end user experience. The bounds of systems are only where you draw the line for yourself, on your team, and within your organization. Keep dreaming and let your imagination be your guide.

CHAPTER 2

Design System Fundamentals

One of the biggest misconceptions about design systems is that they're a tangible, particular thing. Instead, design systems represent a combination of things. They are ecosystems, and ecosystems are hard to point to.

It's like trying to show someone a coral reef. You might take them to the beach and point vaguely toward the ocean. You're not pointing at anything in particular but the combination of elements: water, sand, land, rock, polyps, etc.—so many other parts that contribute to the whole. Without even one of these things, a coral reef is less of itself. So, too, are design systems.

Out of curiosity, I asked people on Twitter how they might point to their design system,[1] and I received dozens of different answers (Figure 2.1). No one individual was correct, but together, they all were.

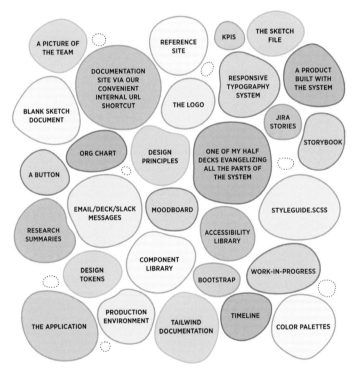

FIGURE 2.1

A design system is an ecosystem consisting of lots of different parts.

1   Dan Mall [@danmall], "If someone said to you, 'Show me your design system,' what's the first thing you'd pull up?" *Twitter*, April 6, 2020, **https://twitter.com/ danmall/status/1247285170396422145**

Word Nerds Unite!

Despite the countless articles, books, videos, courses, and other content about design systems on the internet, part of the challenge of understanding them is that the digital design industry generally doesn't agree on a shared definition. Here are a few different takes on what a design system is:

> A set of connected patterns and shared practices, coherently organized to serve the purposes of a digital product.
>
> —Alla Kholmatova, UX + interaction designer

> A design system offers a library of visual style, components, and other concerns documented and released by an individual, team, or community as code and design tools so that adopting products can be more efficient and cohesive.
>
> —Nathan Curtis, design system evangelist, EightShapes

> A design system [is] the official story of how your organization designs and builds digital interfaces.
>
> —Brad Frost, front-end designer

> A design system is any set of decisions governed across an organization.
>
> —Hayley Hughes, design director, Nike

> The components are the trees. The design system is the forest.
>
> —Jeremy Keith, web developer

All of these things are accurate! The challenge comes from the fact that the root words—"design" and "system"—are each broad. Let's examine where they come from.

"Design" is particularly problematic because it's both a noun and a verb. It started as a verb in the late 14th century with the Latin word designare, which means to "make an identifying mark." The word evolved into a noun as well in the late 16th century with the French word desseign, which means "making a plan with a purpose."

The word "system" emerged in the early 17th century in the Latin word "systema" meaning "an arrangement" and the Greek word "systema" meaning "an organized whole compounded of parts."

Put them together and you have something close to the idea of "an organized arrangement for a particular purpose." That could apply to anything!

Different Kinds of Design Systems

Rather than trying to define design systems outright in order to determine what is and isn't one, be broader and more inclusive about defining design systems. No gatekeeping here! It's a fruitful exercise to identify a few different types of design systems. In relation to digital product work, here are the seven common kinds of design systems:

1. Design systems as brand identities and visual languages
2. Design systems as projects
3. Design systems as tools and templates
4. Design systems as a digital product
5. Design systems as a process
6. Design systems as a service
7. Design systems as a practice

Design Systems as Brand Identities and Visual Languages

Visual languages are one of the oldest kinds of design systems. Humans have reused symbols to communicate meaning from cave paintings as early as 38,000 BCE to the Sumerians' alphabet in 3000 B.C. to movable type in 6th century China to Gutenberg's modern printing press in the 1400s to the email you probably sent a few hours ago. Brands develop visual identities that they reuse to establish themselves in the minds of their consumers. For example, a specific shade of blue reminds people of high-end jewelry retailer Tiffany & Co. (Figure 2.2). A simple bottle silhouette makes you salivate for an ice-cold Coca-Cola (Figure 2.3). People know a phrase on a T-shirt set in Futura Extra Bold Condensed is a Nike shirt without many other signals (Figure 2.4). Visual languages are an important and prevalent kind of design system in our brand-saturated world.

FIGURE 2.2
The iconic Tiffany Blue® is a significant part of the Tiffany & Co. brand identity.

FIGURE 2.3
A simple bottle silhouette paired with a specific shade of red screams Coca-Cola.

FIGURE 2.4
Setting text in Futura Extra Bold Condensed feels like a Nike shirt even before seeing the logo.

Design Systems as Projects

Within a digital design context, many design systems start as a simple project with a deadline and some desired output, usually borne out of the desire for more efficiency. These often look like a manager or supervisor granting permission and extra time to one or more of their direct reports to create some output like a UI kit or a component library of reusable parts with the hope that it will speed up or simplify the next similar project.

Design Systems as Tools and Templates

Particularly good for service providers like freelancers, studios, and agencies that do work that they deliver to others, tools and templates are design systems that are designed to ultimately be detached from their original source and given away to take root elsewhere. These tools and templates could be things like boilerplate contracts and agreements, Keynote and PowerPoint templates, or some generic code files that every project starts with.

HTML5 Boilerplate[2] is a great example of a design system as a tool: created at a central source, it's designed for others to take and modify for their needs (Figure 2.5). The creators call it "delete-key friendly," in that it contains more than you'll probably need, and the process of making it your own involves removing parts that aren't applicable to your use case.

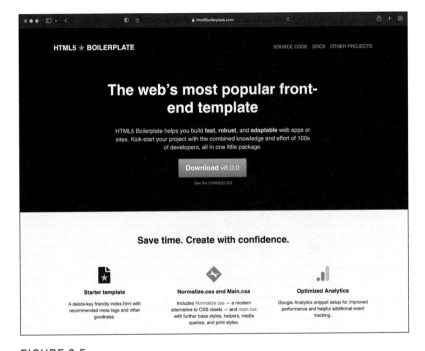

FIGURE 2.5
The HTML5 Boilerplate is a simple template for quickly building web pages that adhere to best practices.

A quick way to employ a design system of tools and templates is to use someone else's. While a design system as a project typically involves the creation of a tool or template, you could certainly purchase a paid tool or start with an open-source one.

---

2 "HTML5 Boilerplate," https://html5boilerplate.com/

Design Systems as Digital Products

In digital design, products are pieces of software that usually get iterated upon over time. They typically have one person or a small team dedicated to improving them, which often means there's an amount of money over time allocated to maintenance costs and compensating employees. (This is the kind of design system you're probably reading this book to learn more about.)

Shopify's Polaris design system is a great example of a design system that's a digital product (Figure 2.6). There are people who work at Shopify whose job it is to work on Polaris full-time. The "What's New" section outlines recent changes entitled "Version 10 typography," which implies that there have been nine prior versions that have been iterated through over time!

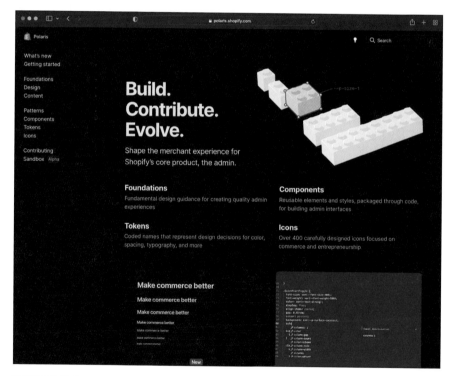

FIGURE 2.6

Shopify's Polaris design system is a digital product that helps Shopify employees build experiences for their merchant customers.

A common characteristic of design systems as products are that they have roadmaps for improvement for the near- to long-term future. This is really what sets a design system as a *product* apart from a design system as a *project*. Projects typically have a deadline and a deliverable, and then they're done. Products are never finished. Consider version-control service GitHub as an example of a digital product. Founded in 2008, GitHub employees have been making their product better for more than a decade, with no sign of stopping. In fact, they've made their roadmap public so that anyone can see what they plan to do in the short-term and long-term (Figure 2.7). Like GitHub, design systems that are products are on a quest to continually improve their product for the foreseeable future.

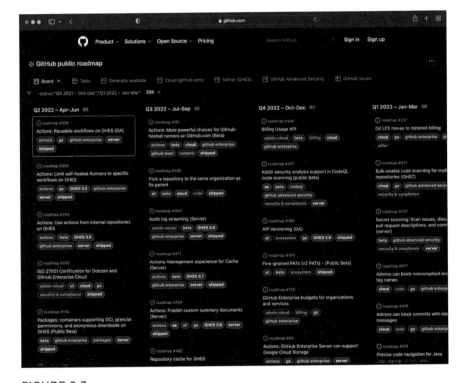

FIGURE 2.7
GitHub makes their roadmap public so that anyone can see what features will be worked on and released in the near future.

Design Systems as a Process

Some design systems aren't a tangible thing. For many organizations, a design system can be a specific way of doing design and product that everyone can adopt and rally around.

Design sprints are a great example of a design system as a process. Popularized by the team at Google's venture fund GV, a design sprint is a five-day process for answering critical business questions through design, prototyping, and testing ideas with customers (Figure 2.8). Agnostic of any specific customer or use case, the GV team uses their design sprint system to help their portfolio companies design new products and explore new markets.

FIGURE 2.8
The GV 5-day sprint is a process that can be effective for any company they take it to.

There are many different kinds of product and design processes that can be adopted as design systems, like double diamonds, spiral models, Lean, and many more. The key to treating them as design systems is making it a shared way of working on your team or at your organization.

Design Systems as a Service

Some organizations treat a design system as a service: a collaborative, interdisciplinary, holistic approach to create experiences that meet a host of needs. Rather than this kind of design system being a tangible thing or an approach, a design system as a service often manifests as a group of people that can be utilized as supplementary knowledge or additional resources. This can be an internal team that gets brought in for special reasons, or it can be a third-party like a consultancy or agency.

An entire branch of a company can be an example of a design system as a service, like a design operations organization. But beware: a design operations organization (DesignOps) can also be the umbrella organization that a design system team sits within. At this level, definitions get really blurry, so focus less on what this is and instead on what value it might provide.

Design Systems as a Practice

On his blog, yoga teacher James Happe describes the difference between *doing* yoga and *practicing* yoga.[3] He talks about doing yoga as something that anyone can do. It can be fun. It can be light. It can be part of a weekly schedule as rarely or often as you prefer.

Practicing yoga, however, is "more about the effort than the result...It requires an active, participatory learning on the part of the student where the instructions are only internalised (sic) through questioning, experimentation, application, and reflection. [It] requires wholehearted attention."

Design systems can be practices, too. Design systems as a practice aren't about a particular artifact, tool, technology, or process. Instead, they're about a shared, collaborative effort that can bring the otherwise disparate disciplines of product, design, and engineering together in harmony.

---

3   James Happe, "The Difference Between Practicing Yoga and Doing Yoga," September 22, 2014, **https://jameshappeyoga.co.za/practicing-yoga-doing-yoga/**

Whichever design system—or combination of them—you're pursuing, you have to do it repeatedly to get good at it. The more you use a tool, the better you utilize it. The more you employ a process, the more familiar it becomes. Design systems that aren't a practice run the risk of quickly becoming dormant, so make sure you're setting aside time to practice using whatever kind of design system you choose.

Choose Your Own Design System Adventure

Every time you begin or continue design system work, declare and decide which one you're working on. This is especially important when you work with a team, as you can accidentally be pursuing different goals without knowing it.

For the purposes of the rest of this book, I'll teach you how to start, grow, and maintain a design system as a product and as a practice. These kinds of design systems stand to reap major rewards for some of the world's largest organizations working at the grandest scales, so it stands to reason that building momentum here would be difficult. Fear not! Understanding what kind of design system you're working on is the first step, and you'll soon see some movement that will start to pick up speed.

Questions for Reflection

- What kinds of design systems do you have experience with? Which are new to you?
- What kind or combination of design systems does your organization have? Is there a different kind or combination that would work better?
- How can you continue to articulate to your team the kind of design system you're pursuing so that you're all working toward the same goal?

CHAPTER 3

The Parts of a Design System Product

The first automobile ever mass-produced was the Ford Model T, created by the Ford Motor Company in 1908. It had little more than an engine, a transmission, a suspension, wheels, and a body. More than a century later, today's cars are much more modern, sophisticated, and advanced than the Model T. Some modern cars automatically turn the windshield wipers on when they detect moisture. Some automatically dim the headlights when another car approaches. Some cars even drive themselves.

Yet, despite these advances and the major differences, it's safe to assume that it wouldn't be too difficult for a driver from today to drive the Model T. Today's cars have the same basic construction: an engine, a transmission, a suspension, wheels, and a body. Because of these standard parts, even new drivers can sit in very different kinds of cars manufactured across many decades and get acclimated in just a few minutes because the parts are fairly common.

The same is true of design systems. Every design system is unique because every organization is, but the same set of standard parts tend to appear from system to system. This means that, if you've learned to use one design system, you can get acclimated to most other design systems fairly quickly.

The Most Common Parts of a Design System

The most common parts of a design system product tend to be naturally aligned to what designers and engineers need in their everyday work. This includes a few tools and assets, some instructions on how to use them, and a few ways to communicate all of it to a broader audience. Many design systems products feature these six common parts (Figure 3.1):

- A UI kit
- A component library
- Guidelines
- A reference website
- Design tokens
- Digital products, e.g. websites and applications

Let's explore and dissect each of these parts.

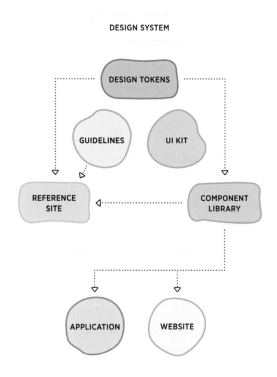

DESIGN SYSTEM

FIGURE 3.1
The six most common pieces of a design system product are shown here.

UI Kit

When many people think about design systems, they picture a UI (user interface) kit, a file typically made in a design tool like Figma or Sketch that displays all the individual components as if they were spread across a table (Figure 3.2).

FIGURE 3.2
Tetrisly is an example of a popular UI kit.

UI kits are useful, but they're only a piece of a design system product, not the entire thing. Prioritizing UI kits higher than the other parts is one of the biggest culprits of why design system products don't get fully adopted throughout an organization. In fact, a UI kit may be the least important part of a design system product ecosystem.

Over the last few years, the design industry has seen a renaissance of sorts in design tooling in applications like Figma and Sketch. The danger that accompanies this revitalization of powerful design tools is to use them for more than is actually useful.

In his keynote address at company conference Config Europe 2020,[1] Figma CEO Dylan Field introduced the new Variants feature by walking through a file that showed the Settings page of the Spotify mobile application. He described the problem designers face in creating a page like this that can show different states of the page with certain items toggled on and others toggled off. He said, "If I was going to try and prototype this in Figma today, I'd have to make [a] monstrosity, because I'd have to think about all of the possible combinations, which is something like 26. We started prototyping it out to see if it could work, but we stopped halfway through because there are better things to do with our time."

Although the new Figma Variants feature certainly makes it easier to prototype that kind of Settings screen, the hidden toxicity that snuck in is that it makes designers think that this work is even worth doing in the first place. Rather than actually creating work that increases customer value, designers squander their efforts on polishing UI kits and wiring up Settings screens in a design tool instead of a true software environment. (I'll explore worthwhile work effort in more detail in Chapter 7, "Roles and Responsibilities.")

Component Library

Engineers need their own equivalent of a UI kit, but in code, as opposed to a design tool. That's typically known as a *component library* or a *pattern library*. (I'll refer to it as a "component library" for the rest of this book, but the terms are generally interchangeable.) Components are reusable snippets of code, so a component library is a collection of code snippets where you can browse examples and references for implementing into a codebase.

---

1 "Config Europe 2020," YouTube, September 17, 2020, **www.youtube.com/ watch?v=lWy4fB3G9Gc**

Design systems that are products need some way of connecting reusable component code to digital products that end-customers interact with, and component libraries are the most common way to do that. That's why the majority of most design system products are component libraries, followed by the guidelines that accompany the components.

Google's Material Design is more of a methodology than a product, much of which you can read about on the Material Design reference website (Figure 3.3). However, at the time of this writing, the web component library for Material is a simple GitHub repository of components with very little documentation,[2] so other third-party companies have taken the Material Design methodology and created their own component libraries for it (Figure 3.4).

FIGURE 3.3
Material Design is more than just a component library. It's an entire methodology for designing and building digital products that feel inherently like Google products.

---

2   Material Design Team, "Material Web," GitHub, https://github.com/material-components/material-web#readme

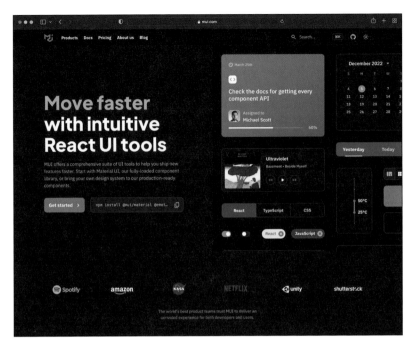

FIGURE 3.4
MUI (Material UI) is a third-party library that features coded components based around the Material Design approach.

Because the design system product industry is so young, there are many emerging and promising ideas in this space. One to watch is the effort of tools like Bit (Figure 3.5), favoring more of a micro front-end approach. Their proposition is to move teams away from building monolithic, organization-centric design systems and more toward, in their own words, "component-driven apps composed of independent components built by autonomous teams working side by side."

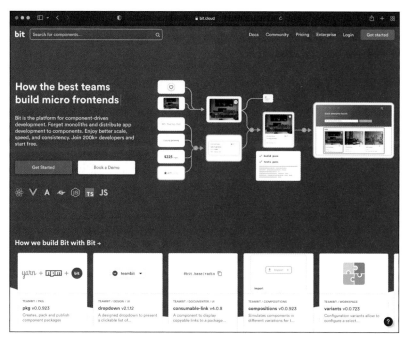

FIGURE 3.5

Bit is an open-source toolchain for component-driven software.

Guidelines

Every good design system has *guidelines*, suggestions or rules to follow for how to best use any given design system. Good guidelines tell you what and what not to do. Design system guidelines often take the form of principles or user experience best practices.

At first glance, this might seem like the same thing as a reference website, but not all guidelines or documentation need to live on a reference site—nor should they! The best guidelines help designers and engineers at the point in their work where they need it, often called "just-in-time" documentation. For example, designer Mike Wilson has built a Figma plug-in called *Gist*[3] (Figure 3.6) that lets you "view attached documentation without leaving your working file." The documentation for a component is right there in your view as you're working on it in your working environment.

---

3   Mike Wilson, "Gist," Figma Community, **www.figma.com/community/ plugin/1073059820691713754/Gist**

FIGURE 3.6

The Gist plug-in for Figma brings documentation right into the design environment.

Reference Website

UI kits, component libraries, and guidelines are typically compiled together in a reference website or reference site (also known as a *style guide site*). A reference site is a visible manifestation of a design system, typically a URL that displays both the full component library and a set of guidelines. Most design system reference websites are largely documentation references. (This misses a large opportunity, which I expound on in Chapter 10, "Evangelism Never Stops.") Unencumbered access to the documentation needed to use a design system plays a big part in how much that system is used. If the system is difficult to use or a practitioner can't figure out how to use it, they're often content to find another resource that's easier for them, which is likely a big part of why many folks look to Bootstrap or Material Design over creating their own design system or even using the one they already have.

For many oft-admired design systems, the reference site is most people's entry point into it. When people talk about Shopify's Polaris, they're often referring to what they see at **https://polaris.shopify.com/**. When people talk about IBM's Carbon Design System, they're often referring to what they see at **https://carbondesignsystem.com/**. When people talk about Salesforce's Lightning Design System, they're often referring to what they see at **www.lightningdesignsystem.com/**. For all of these examples, the reference sites are completely public, i.e., anyone with an internet connection can view them.

There are many benefits to a completely public reference website. Front-end designer Brad Frost is explicit about this in his book *Atomic Design*. His subsection about making a design system public is part of a larger section called "Make It Visible," within a chapter entitled, "Maintaining Design Systems." And rightly so! Making a design system public is a crucial part of understanding how to keep it managed and maintained. Brad explains that making a design system public:

- **Increases its visibility**, which therefore increases the likelihood of use.

- **Creates accountability** by demonstrating a commitment to a product dedicated to consistency and reusability.

- **Helps recruiting** by publicly signaling values that attract like-minded individuals to join the organization.

With all the advantages of a completely public reference site, why aren't all design system reference sites public? In theory, there's not much to making a design system public. After all, if there's one core skill a web designer or web developer should have, it's taking some HTML files and putting them on a server that has an associated URL. (FTP, anyone?)

What prevents a design system from being public? In short: business. If you work at an organization with enough sprawl to warrant a design system, chances are high that there's an IT process for getting any site deployed. That process likely includes authentication of some form, and launching something publicly is one of the most risk-loaded actions you can undertake, so it has the most amount of rigor attached to it. I've seen this process take months or even be blocked altogether. All of that can be a deterrent to even attempting to have a public design system.

LinkedIn senior UX lead Nate Whitson makes it plain: "It's non-trivial to be able to share all of your documentation publicly." Nate expounds on that statement to say that sharing information outside a company means you need additional context for the uninitiated, which amounts to extra overhead on what you might write, design, and document.

But "public" isn't an all-or-nothing kind of decision. The accepted definition of a "public design system" tends to refer to a design system with both a public reference site and an open-source code library. GitHub Head of Design Diana Mounter describes the different degrees of how a design system can be public:

- **Public documentation only:** The reference site is accessible to all, but the code itself is hidden away.

- **Open-source code library:** Not only is the code public, but people are free to request features and contribute back (with acceptance of contributions at the maintainers' discretion).

- **Open-source documentation:** People can modify and contribute only to the documentation, not the design system code itself.
- **Downloadable:** Typically in the form of a zip file, this can allow for a downloadable version of the design system that's different from the code that maintainers actually work with.
- **Publish the component library:** You could publish a read-only version of your component library—Storybook, Pattern Lab, Fractal, etc.—to a URL that all can see.

Software engineer Ryan DeBeasi shares how he's split the difference in the past. "We didn't have permission to make our design system public, so we did the next best thing: we treated it like a small open-source project within the organization," which reinforces the idea that making a design system public has many different flavors.

A PRIMER ON DESIGN TOKENS

 Esther Cheran is the chief product officer and co-founder of Hyma, a company building the next generation of tooling in the design systems and design tokens space. She's also the co-creator of the widely used Tokens Studio for Figma. I asked her a few questions about her experience with design tokens and how they help amplify the efficacy of a design system.

What is a design token?
Design tokens are the smallest design decisions that encapsulate a brand identity. Examples of a design token are design decisions like border radius, border width, and background fill of a button.

What's your experience with design tokens?
I started using design tokens to build a tokenized Design System, which eventually became the Headless Design System. During that time, I was using Tokens Studio created by Jan Six very heavily and eventually started contributing to the plug-in and became one of the co-creators.

I was pushing the boundaries of how design tokens can be used to build completely headless design systems and the concept really took off with a lot of other teams building multibrand design systems.

How do design tokens help designers?
Design tokens are now becoming available to designers to actually use in their design process through tools like Tokens Studio and soon

Design Tokens

Design tokens aren't technically a requirement of a design system in the same way that guidelines or a component library are, but many teams are using or starting to use them to make a design system even more useful and powerful. As defined by the Design Tokens W3C Community Group, a design token is "the single source of truth to name and store a design decision, distributed so teams can use it across design tools and coding languages." A common use for design tokens is to centralize design and brand attributes across multiple platforms like web, iOS, Android, and more.

Digital Products: Websites and Applications

The last piece is the most important: *digital products*! These could be websites, native mobile applications, kiosks, touchscreen

native implementations in design tools. Because of this, designers have a direct feedback loop with tokens making maintenance of the system a lot easier and also making design consistency less prone to human error.

How do design tokens help engineers?

Design tokens take out the guesswork in interpreting designs from designers. Any minor changes in the look of the components can be done by designers without having to allocate developer resources.

How do design tokens help team members who aren't designers or engineers?

Design tokens give everyone a single source of truth to work from. For example, brand teams can visualize and quickly prototype how the brand would look using tokenized mock-ups.

What advice would you give to someone who has never used design tokens before?

Design tokens should be used as per the requirement of your project. You might not need a complicated design token architecture with several layers of token sets and themes if you are building a single brand design system. A simple token architecture would suffice. On the other hand, a multibrand design system that caters to different platforms might need a more complicated multitiered architecture.

apps—essentially, any application that lives on a screen. Without a real digital product for someone to use, a design system is just a theoretical exercise, a tool that never gets pulled out of its toolbox. The more products that use the design system, the more evident the design system's usefulness becomes. And there you have it: all of the parts of a design system product!

The Sum of Its Parts

A design system is the sum of its parts. It's the whole thing, not any one piece in particular.

Each individual part of a design system helps a specific discipline. UI kits help designers to design faster and better. Component libraries help engineers to code faster and better. Those tools help primarily with process.

But a design system is a tool for an entire team, not a particular discipline. Design systems help product teams deliver software to their customers faster and better. Design systems aren't a process tool; they're a delivery product.

Design Systems Are About Connectedness

Most of the conversation about design systems tends to center around components: how to architect them, compose them, combine them, and the like. In her book *Thinking in Systems*, environmental scientist, educator, and writer Donella Meadows outlines what is and isn't a system. She says, "A conglomeration without any particular interconnections or functions [is not a system]...stop dissecting elements and start looking for the interconnections, the relationships that hold the elements together."[4]

What's more important than the individual components within a design system is how they relate to one another. Look for what's shared, what's common, the connections between the components.

True design systems are connected. Design and engineering need to be connected to product. How do you do that exactly? Read on!

---

4   Donella H. Meadows, *Thinking in Systems* (White River Jct., VT: Chelsea Green Publishing, 2008), 14.

Component Libraries vs. Design Systems

Part of the confusion around design systems happens because some terms and concepts are interchangeable while others aren't. It's difficult to know which is which. "Component library" and "pattern library" generally mean the same thing. "Alert" components are often called "notification" or "toast" components. But "pills" and "badges" are very different, even though they might look identical.

Perhaps the most common conflation of terms occurs within the difference between a component library and a design system. These terms cannot and should not be used interchangeably, because they're very different things, even though they seem comparable at first glance.

How to Use a Component Library

Bootstrap was originally conceived as "simple and flexible HTML, CSS, and JavaScript for popular user interface components and interactions" (Figure 3.7). From that description, it's unclear whether Bootstrap is a component library or a full design system.

FIGURE 3.7

The Bootstrap website debuted with a handful of common components for designers and developers to use.

The clarity comes from the intended way to use Bootstrap. The two main calls to action at the top of the page are to "View project on GitHub" and "Download Bootstrap." Subsequent versions of the Bootstrap website simplified it even further to only "Download Bootstrap." Tapping that button prompts the download of a ZIP folder containing CSS, icons, and JavaScript files to be copied and pasted into a build.

This is the first clue about whether Bootstrap is a component library or a design system. Downloading files is working with duplicates; it's your own copy of the original set of files. Downloading means you have your own version, which means the version of Bootstrap in your files isn't connected to the official version of Bootstrap anymore. Remember: true design systems are *connected*, so using Bootstrap this way isn't using a design system.

The difference further intensifies as you start to use Bootstrap's components. For example, to use Bootstrap's "Breadcrumb" component, navigate to that "Breadcrumb" page in the "Components" documentation section and copy this code into your build:

```
<nav aria-label="breadcrumb">
    <ol class="breadcrumb">
        <li class="breadcrumb-item"><a href="#">Home</a></li>
        <li class="breadcrumb-item active" aria-current="page">
            Library
        </li>
    </ol>
</nav>
```

Again, as soon as you copy and paste, you're breaking any connection from an original source. For those familiar with Figma, this is the code equivalent of detaching an instance from its original component definition. Component libraries rely mainly on copying and pasting, whereas design systems maintain a connection to the original source.

It's worth noting that there's nothing wrong with using a component library. In fact, component libraries are incredibly useful for the general practice of software development and were partially the precursor to what eventually evolved into the practice of design systems. However, a component library doesn't utilize many of the advantages that a true, connected design system can bring to a product team and an organization.

Imagine if the team that makes Bootstrap releases a new version with updated breadcrumbs. While the updates may be both beneficial and desirable, they might conflict with the customizations you've made to the version you've downloaded and worked with. You're stuck between a choice of retaining the work you've already done or updating it and having to start from scratch.

How to Use a Design System

Contrast that with using something like Material UI, a React-based design system built to implement Google's Material Design aesthetic into products. Tapping "Get Started" or scrolling down on the homepage tells you how to start using Material UI in your build. Unlike Bootstrap, which asks you to download files, Material UI asks you to "install" it. That's a major distinction: component libraries get downloaded, while design systems need to be installed. Let's walk through the details of how that works by way of an example React app to, say, build a dashboard that lets you see your personal finances at a glance.

Open the root of your React app in a Terminal window.

Type `npm install @material-ui/core` at the prompt.

That's it! The design system is now installed as a dependency in your financial dashboard React app. That's a fancy way of saying that this financial dashboard is built on top of the Material UI design system.

You can check that, too, just to make sure. If you open the `package.json` file in the root folder of this project, you'll see these lines:

```
{
    "name": "Example App",
    "version": "5.0.0",
    "private": true,
    "scripts": {
        // build scripts go here
    },
    "dependencies": {
        "@material-ui/core": "^5.0.0-alpha.12",
        "react": "latest"
    }
}
```

Many popular design systems are built on React. What is React, and why is it a good choice for design systems?

Per its official website, React is "a JavaScript library for building user interfaces" (Figure 3.8). It was originally created in 2011 by Facebook software engineer Jordan Walker to make it easier to build complex user interfaces like Facebook's newsfeed. Being the library that powers a highly-trafficked page like Facebook's newsfeed is a heck of a proof-of-concept, so many engineers quickly adopted React as their library of choice.

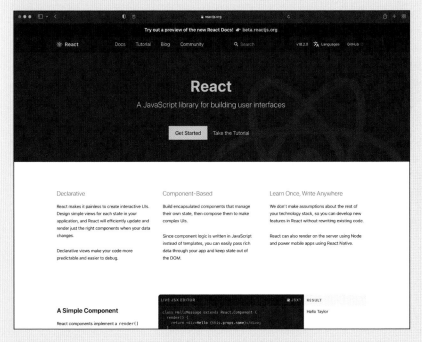

FIGURE 3.8
React is a popular library for building user interfaces.

The heart of React's allure is that it's a component-based library. It incentivizes writing code in a way that's reusable and portable, a perfect fit for design systems.

While most of the code examples in this book feature React code, the principles apply to many other component-based libraries like Angular and Vue, even if the syntax varies from library to library.

Line 9 is what you're looking for. Translated to plain speak, this line says your financial dashboard application is *dependent* on Material UI version 5.0.0, release alpha 12. Just like kids are dependent on their parents for a few crucial things, this app is dependent on Material UI. If Material UI didn't exist, your dashboard would be incomplete. That's the link back to the original design system. That's the connectedness that Donella Meadows was talking about.

The benefit that connection gets you is real-time updates both ways. If the Material UI team makes a change to breadcrumbs, you get them for free the second you decide you want them. All you have to do is type `npm update @material-ui/core` in your Terminal. That will edit the line in `package.json` you just looked at from `"@material-ui/core": "^5.0.0-alpha.12"` to `"@material-ui/core": "^5.0.1-alpha.13."` No overriding will happen. No erased changes. No redoing work. The software does all the merging, keeping your old work while integrating the new stuff, and you are none the wiser.

If you make a change to the breadcrumbs on your side and decide it might be applicable to everyone else that uses Material UI, there's also a way for you to contribute that back to the Material UI library for others to use, assuming you have the proper permissions to be able to do that. (I'll go into more detail about contribution in Chapter 5, "Pilots—The Best Way to Start and Sustain a Design System.")

NOTE WEB VS. NATIVE

> This is how design systems products for the web get installed and used. Design systems products for native mobile platforms like iOS and Android have slightly different steps, but the general idea is the same.

Connect the Entire Digital Ecosystem

A true, connected design system maintains a link from the financial dashboard app to the design system itself so that they're always intact and always able to be in sync. The real power of all this is that it's not just one site that can be linked to the design system, but all of an organization's digital products can maintain a connection between itself, the design system, and all the other products in that ecosystem. When you install the design system as a dependency in every website and application, each instance is connected to the system—and, therefore, connected to each other.

One of the first big pitfalls that design system teams at an organization encounter is thinking they have a true design system product when, in fact, all they have are design system tools like UI kits or component libraries, and they don't know the difference. Worse still, they're baffled about why it's so difficult to scale the kind of efficiency and consistency that true design system products and practices bring.

Now that you know the difference, spread the word!

Questions for Reflection

Take these questions back to your teams of designers, engineers, and product managers in order to help identify design system gaps:

- Do you have a UI kit, a component library, a true design system, or something else at your organization?
- Whichever one you have, how did it get that way? (Understanding how something came to be may help unlock how to get it to progress.)
- What links or connections are you maintaining between your digital products and your design system?
- How can you move your organization toward a more connected system? If you already have a connected system, how can you deepen the commitment to sustaining a true, connected design system?

CHAPTER 4

The Broken Business of "Buy-In"

There's a common narrative about the "right" way to start a design system that almost always ends in failure. Those steps look something like this:

1. **Pitch the project.** Propose a design system initiative to executive leadership to get their buy-in in the form of both conceptual blessing and literal funding to grow a team.

2. **Create the building blocks.** A small team creates foundational components—"the design system"—that all other product teams are prone to implement and use.

3. **Use the system.** Product teams begin using the design system's components in their product work.

4. **Contribute back.** For anything that's not already in the design system, a product team creates it and then contributes it to the design system for other teams to use.

This process almost never works, and teams are left scratching their heads as to why. It's because this plan is entirely wishful thinking, and not at all realistic.

"Make System, Use System" Is a Fantasy

The core idea behind the way most people think to create a design system is this: first you make the system, and then you use the system you made. So simple! My kids sometimes think this way: "Dad, you put the old stuff you don't want out on the lawn for a yard sale, and then you make a lot of money from it." Duh! All we need to do is make a really good design system, and people will use it. Duh! This reeks of a naïve "If you build it, they will come" strategy.

The pitfalls are in the details, and they exist in every step. These steps don't work because every step is individually difficult; each has a high potential for failure.

Getting Design System Buy-in Is Often Pitching Vaporware

Proposing a design system initiative to leadership is tough because the design system you're pitching doesn't exist yet—it's vaporware. As of this writing, there are three billion Google search results on "getting buy-in for a design system." The top results share similar advice: prepare your elevator pitch, define the pain, compile projections about the business value of design systems and their typical return on investment, show a plan on getting from zero to up-and-running, and communicate your progress to your stakeholders often. With these pillars, you're bound to get leadership excited and full funding to make your design system dreams a reality.

It's an attractive concept that rarely works.

Perhaps the venture capital-funded, startup unicorn world we live in has fooled enough of us into thinking that, if only our pitch is strong enough, people will invest, sight unseen. But, in the same way that a VC is more likely to invest once a startup has found traction—that is, a critical mass of people are already using the product—executive leadership will be much more likely to bless a design system initiative after people are steadily using a design system. Until then, you're just crossing your fingers for a leadership team that has a high tolerance for risk, a rarity these days.

Abstract Design Systems Are Difficult to Make

Creating foundational building blocks is difficult because it's an abstract exercise. Even the supposedly simple task of creating a color palette is fraught with difficult questions to answer in abstraction, which is why most design system color palettes end up including every hue of the rainbow and multiple shades of grayscale with little guidance on how to use any of them.

You end up with a system that's more "book smart" than "street smart." It's like telling a kid that they must learn the ins and outs of music theory before they can jam on a familiar tune. Music theory knowledge would certainly be helpful, but it severely delays the joys of being able to play a song and impress your friends.

When design system work is done in a vacuum and a design system team doesn't have specific use cases, their strategy seems to be something akin to "let's provide as many elements as product teams might need at any point," leading to bloated design systems. In trying to create a design system that gets used by anyone and everyone, they actually create a design system for no one in particular.

Good Luck Convincing Someone to Adopt a New Tool

"But Dan!" you object. "You're being so pessimistic! Surely, it's possible to create something that would be valuable for product teams to use." It's true: there are teams that manage to get past this stage and emerge with potentially useful components that are able to appropriately balance flexibility and specificity.

Now it's time to get teams to use this new system. This usually poses the next big blocker: convincing someone to adopt a new tool—or generally just to do anything new—is difficult! You're asking product teams to renounce their familiar tools and employ yours instead. How do they know they can trust it? Will it work for them? Will they know how to use it? How steep is the learning curve?

The typical proposal that design system teams give is that their newly created system of building blocks is objectively better than other tools, and that it will create more consistency across all of the organization's websites and applications because it has the brand's color palette and typography built in, among other things.

The challenge isn't that this stance is wrong; it's that the stance is irrelevant, at least right now. It's answering questions that haven't been asked. The design system team is trying to solve problems of consistency, but product teams are mostly trying to meet their already aggressive deadlines. Anything that might slow them down—like investing time and mental space in learning a new tool—is considered a nonstarter.

This step is particularly exasperating because you're literally fighting the science here. Behaviorally speaking, humans tend to follow the principle of least effort (or Zipf's Law), which says that, given the choice, animals, people, and even well-designed machines will choose the path of least resistance as a way of conserving as much energy as possible. That path is usually continuing to do what's currently being done. Pragmatically, teams are generally predisposed to stick to their current practices by default, a major hurdle in trying to get them to adopt your new design system.

Product Teams Don't Contribute to Design Systems

One of the biggest complaints I hear from design system teams is that their product or feature teams don't contribute to the design system. Of course, they don't! It's difficult enough getting them to adopt the risk of using a new design system into their current workflow.

There are two main reasons why product teams don't contribute to their organization's design system(s):

- **Too many new things.** According to a paper published by a Duke University researcher in 2006,[1] more than 40 percent of a person's daily actions are driven by habits. Introducing too many new tools and processes into a team's standard way of creating products simply won't take.

- **It's not their job.** A product team's job is to make product, not contribute to a design system. Asking a team that's typically understaffed and worried about a deadline to contribute to a design system is exactly why that request moves to the bottom of a backlog.

In the next chapter, I'll show you how to make contribution a much more natural and automatic part of a design system workflow.

Questions for Reflection

- Do you have buy-in on your design system? If so, how did you get it? If not, how can you get it?
- If the usual business of buy-in is broken, what might be a better way? Note your answer now and compare it to what you learn is a better way a few chapters from now.

---

1   David T. Neal, Wendy Wood, and Jeffrey Quinn, "Habits—A Repeat Performance," Neuron, (2006), http://web.archive.org/web/20110526144503/http://dornsife.usc.edu/wendywood/research/documents/Neal.Wood.Quinn.2006.pdf

CHAPTER 5

Pilots—The Best Way to Start and Sustain a Design System

Instead of employing a fingers-crossed, "make system, use system" strategy, piloting a design system by way of product work is a much more successful strategy for creating—or recreating—a design system at an organization.

Consider the way a television series is sold to a network. The show's creators don't simply ask for a budget to make a show. They make something first. They make one episode—a pilot—designed to gauge how successful more episodes and seasons might be. That pilot is intended to prototype characters, interactions, dialogue, scenes, and more to justify further episodes and seasons of the show. The pilot for ABC's hit drama *Lost* dropped viewers directly into the show just moments after a plane crash on a mysterious island. The audience got a glimpse into many of the characters and some hints that everything on the island might not be what it seemed. They were hooked! Bring on more episodes!

The point of having a design system is to improve the process and output of making digital products. But, before investing significant time and money to establish a full design system and an associated practice, it's worthwhile to test out what kind of design system you'll need, in order to build confidence that you can create more products like that in the future. The best way to pilot a design system is to make a product with that design system—even if the system doesn't exist yet.

Linking Design System to Product Work

Linking design system work directly to ongoing digital product work is one of the most successful ways to get traction for a design system. Why? Science, of course! Isaac Newton's first law of motion—the law of inertia—says that objects at rest tend to remain at rest. In design-system-speak, that means that an organization without a design system is most likely to continue not having one.

Fortunately, science has the solution, too! The law of inertia also confirms that opposite: objects in motion tend to stay in motion. If you want to get a design system initiative to start moving, hitch it to something that's already moving. What kinds of things are already moving in organizations that make digital products? The digital product creation process! New products and features are always on roadmaps. Teams are already allocated and have funding and executive buy-in to work on those features. Use their momentum as your own!

In digital-centric organizations, there are a handful of inflection points that are perfect boarding platforms for design system work:

- Rebranding
- Replatforming
- Re-org
- Content or migration
- Merging with or acquiring another company

What do these events have in common? These are points where the organization has already committed to a large company-wide change. Hitch your design system quest to those wagons, because they're already on the move. Volunteer your team to tackle this work. This is the kind of work where it's common to hear the sentiment, "While we're doing this, we might as well try to do it as efficiently as we can," which is the perfect gateway to start laying the groundwork for a design system practice.

You don't even have to say the words "design system." In fact, I'd encourage you not to say those words to leadership, because it often feels like a distraction to them. Instead of talking about the tool you're making—a design system—talk more about the outcome of that work.

"Doing work in this way will put us six weeks ahead of schedule."

"See how many fewer bugs we had by reusing code that's already been through QA (quality assurance)?"

"Our velocity has increased over the last few weeks."

You and your team will know that a design system was the vehicle you used to create these kinds of wins, but no one else will be the wiser just yet.

A Design System Pilot Scorecard

Doing design system pilots in a useful order simultaneously improves your product offering while growing your design system. Which begs the question: How do you choose a useful sequence? A well-rounded scorecard can help determine what products best feed a design system, and in what order.

Pull up your organization's roadmap for new products to create, in addition to existing products to touch up or rethink. You can score every product against these eight factors on a scale from 0 (unlikely) to 10 (very likely) to help determine which products make for good design system pilots:

- **Potential for common components.** Does this pilot have many components that can be reused in other products?
- **Potential for common patterns.**[1] Does this pilot have many patterns that can be reused in other products?
- **High-value elements.** Is there a component or pattern with high business value that is the heart of this project?
- **Technical feasibility.** How simple is a technical implementation of the design system? Is a large refactor required?
- **Available champion.** Will someone working on this product see it through and celebrate/evangelize using the design system (and even contributing to it)?
- **Scope.** Is this work accomplishable in our pilot timeframe of [3–4 weeks] (insert your timing here)?
- **Technical independence.** Is the work decoupled enough from other legacy design and code that there are clear start-and-end points?
- **Marketing potential.** Will this work excite others to use the design system?

Once you've scored each new product on your roadmap (Table 5.1), average the scores and order them from highest to lowest. This is the sequence that will best grow your design system. Do the highest score first and the lowest score last. If you've scored this accurately, and you do the highest scoring pilot first, the second pilot should benefit from the work you've done on the first one. And the third would benefit from the second, and so on. The pilots should get easier as you go along, because you should be extracting components and patterns from each pilot, growing the design system constantly.

---

1   In this instance, I'm distinguishing components from patterns, in that components refer to common static elements like buttons and cards while patterns refer to common interaction flows like login and checkout.

TABLE 5.1 AN EXAMPLE DESIGN SYSTEM PILOT SCORECARD

	Flagship .com Website	Native iOS Application	Employee Intranet
Potential for Common Components	7	2	10
Potential for Common Patterns	7	2	10
High-value Elements	4	3	3
Technical Feasibility	2	10	5
Available Champion	8	6	9
Scope	1	10	1
Technical Independence	4	3	8
Marketing Potential	10	10	4
Totals	43	46	50
Average	5.38	5.75	6.25

Another useful thing about this kind of roadmap scoring is that sequencing is often subjective. Sometimes, a powerful or loud product owner picks their pet projects or favorite features to get funding and priority, often under some hand-wavy guise of "business value." A scorecard like this turns that subjectivity into something more objective that can be debated and discussed against agreed-upon criteria. Making good roadmap decisions should be the same as making good design system decisions and vice versa.

Types of Design System Pilots

Just like there are different kinds of TV pilots—premise pilots set up a scenario that may drive the first season, while non-premise pilots spend more time on characters' lives and personalities—design system pilots can vary in type, scale, and scope. The driving question is, "What do we need to be able to make with our design system?" To answer that, each digital product used as a design system pilot should attempt to test something specific. Using a product build to pilot the expressiveness of a design system is a very different pilot than testing how quickly a product can be built.

Here are a few different kinds of pilots you can run depending on what kind of output you're trying to test:

- **The Indiana Jones:** In a scene from *Raiders of the Lost Ark*, adventurous archaeology professor Indiana Jones tries to swap a golden idol with a bag of sand weighing approximately the same amount in hopes no one will notice the change. One of the earliest kinds of pilots worth doing is to refactor a codebase from using custom-built components to ones coming from a central design-system repository. It's a way to establish a connected system where there was previously none. An important aspect of this kind of pilot is to resist the temptation to "improve" anything while you're in there. Don't make design or user experience changes. The big idea with this kind of pilot is that nothing will appear different to an end user.

- **The Facelift:** These pilots are perfect for helping migrate products to a new visual language, especially useful after a big rebrand. If the design system already contains pieces of the new identity, like updated typefaces and color palettes, you can use this kind of pilot to entice product teams to upgrade to the new visual language "for free" just by adopting the design system.

- **The Speed Run:** The point of this kind of pilot is to test how quickly you can create an interface with components from the design system. Choose a feature, page, or product to construct and give yourself a small window of time to complete this pilot. The more of this kind of pilot you can do, the more confidently you can advertise the design system as a major timesaver.

- **The Surrogate:** The best pilots are working on real roadmap items, but sometimes that just isn't feasible due to team availability, tight deadlines, lack of interest, and more. In those scenarios, the design system team can role-play as a product team, building front-end prototypes of current features but with the design system instead. Those prototypes can be made available as a front-end target and example to strive for once the actual product team has the bandwidth.

- **The Perimeter:** Flagship products make the best impression when you tell people they were built on the design system, but they're also the most difficult to line up. Stakeholders are more protective of them, and their roadmaps may be impossible to influence. Take the opposite approach: build the products with the least amount of red tape to be involved with and do as many of them as you can very quickly. When my team and I worked with a hotel chain, we used pilots like the Wi-Fi landing screen and front desk welcome screen, products that got way less stakeholder attention than something like a booking page but actually were seen by guests way more often.

Be creative with the kinds of pilots you run and watch your design system grow naturally!

NOTE NEEDS AND WANTS

A semantic difference to be sure, but it's important that the question driving a pilot is "What do we *need* to be able to make with our design system?" and not "What do we *want* to be able to make with our design system?" If the question were the latter, it would be too easy to answer, "Anything and everything!" This well-intentioned sentiment is often what leads teams to create design system graveyards of too many components that no one needs and not enough components that are actually needed.

A simple but useful guideline here is to create a design system that your organization needs, even if it's not the design system that everyone wants. How do you know what people at your organization need? Ask them!

Multiple, Concurrent Pilots

It's sensible to think that working on one pilot at a time is a reasonable way to grow a design system. Resist that urge. Your first pilot will probably go pretty well. Then you'll realize that, unless you got lucky, very few of your components that came from the first pilot work well in the second, because you didn't have the second use case in mind yet.

If you eventually want your design system to simultaneously power your interfaces for web, native mobile applications, and lean-back experience, you have to simultaneously pilot powering interfaces for web, native mobile applications, and lean-back experiences. It might be messy to wrangle, but it will reflect the reality of what you're trying to do. If you can't support it in a piloting environment, that's a helpful indicator that your design system might not be able to support multiple teams across all of those platforms in the future. Pilots should give the team a taste of what's ahead and the confidence that they can do it.

To that end, a good starting point is to work on three pilots at the same time, using your pilot scorecard to identify three in sequence. Across science, religion, philosophy, and psychology, three is a special number. Three is the smallest number to see patterns emerge (see sidebar: "Three Times Is a Pattern"). Three concurrent pilots give you ample range and variety without being too overwhelming.

That means the ideal piloting setup is to have four teams running simultaneously (Figure 5.1):

1. Product 1 team
2. Product 2 team
3. Product 3 team
4. Design system team

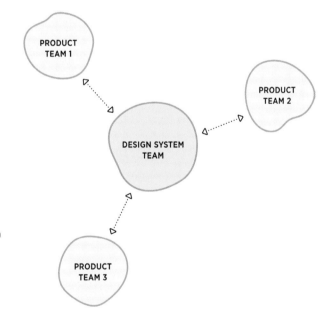

FIGURE 5.1
The beauty and the challenge of a design system ecosystem is managing at least four concurrent workstreams.

Coordinating four teams to work on four independent products that still have overlap is no small feat. Luckily, you can treat the idea and scope of a pilot as liberally as you please. A pilot could be a full-on product with many different components and pages and screens and states, like an intranet, a dashboard, or a shopping cart. But it doesn't have to be. A pilot could also be one page or feature of a product, like a pricing table or embeddable video. Heck, a pilot could be a particularly complex component, like a calculator, a tab set, or a header.

Remember: the important part of a pilot is that it answers the question, "What do we need to be able to make with our design system?" As long as it accomplishes that outcome, give yourself permission to dial down how much you're biting off at a time in order to rack up some wins and confidence for the team.

THREE TIMES IS A PATTERN

Ian Fleming is the author of the James Bond series of spy novels. In his book *Goldfinger*, one of the characters says to James Bond, "Once is happenstance. Twice is coincidence. The third time, it's enemy action." In other words, it's only after the third time that you have enough confidence that the pattern is on purpose.

So, when do you contribute a component to the design system? When three or more teams need it or are using it.

Design systems exist to solve common problems. Less than three instances isn't common enough to be worthwhile work to warrant a design system team's attention. Design systems are a tool for scale. Spending time on one-offs (and two-offs) isn't working at scale, but three or more starts will get you in that territory.

If it's good enough for 007, it's probably good enough for you.

Improving the System as You Use It

There's a scene in *Harry Potter and the Half-Blood Prince* where teenage wizard Harry and his friend Ron arrive late to their first class of the year of "Advanced Potion Making." Harry tells Professor Slughorn that they don't have textbooks yet, so Slughorn sends them into the closet to get some.

There are two books left: a brand new one and an old, beat-up, used one (Figure 5.2). Ron and Harry fight over it, and Harry gets stuck with the old one.

FIGURE 5.2
Trick question: Would you choose the brand-new textbook or the old used one?

The first assignment given to the class is to brew an acceptable draft of Living Death, and whomever can do this will win a vial of Liquid Luck as a prize. Slughorn says the recipe for Living Death is found on page 10 of the textbook, but he also warns that only once did a student ever manage to brew a potion of sufficient quality to claim the prize. (Foreshadowing!)

All of the students struggle, but Harry discovers that his old textbook—labeled property of "the Half-Blood Prince"—is full of notes written in the margin that show how to successfully brew this potion (Figure 5.3). The notes share tips like, "Crush with blade" instead of "cut" like the instructions say. Or use 13 beans instead of 12.

With his annotated textbook, Harry's the only one who manages to make the potion successfully and win the prize. It's almost like cheating to have someone who's done it before tell you how to do it successfully.

Many teams approach making a design system like writing a textbook. They write down the ideal way to build a product in theory. They try to guess what the perfect card component for everyone would be.

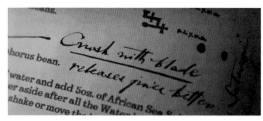

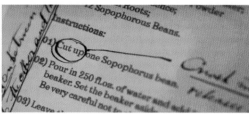

FIGURE 5.3
Notes from someone who has done what you're currently attempting to do are invaluable.

But that's just a spec. It hasn't really been proven yet. That's why piloting is so useful. A design system isn't writing a spec beforehand. It's doing something successfully and documenting it while you're doing it.

Front-end designer Brad Frost says a design system is "the official story of how an organization designs and builds digital interfaces."[2] Said differently, it's a collection of stories for how teams at this organization have made digital products that highlight the patterns that emerge from seeing all those stories in one place.

Make a cheat sheet for people who create digital products after you have. Crush with blade; don't cut. Use 13 beans, not 12. Inline alerts here, not pop-ups. This shade of teal because it has higher contrast against the background. Not because that could work in the future, but because that has worked in the past.

Stop trying to make a design system by making abstract components. Instead, give your team a use case. Pick a potion to brew like "Living Death." Choose the main product dashboard. Build the new intranet. Put yourself in the shoes of the people trying to use the design system by trying to make something close to what they'd be making. If the design system needs to streamline the process of making intranets in the future, start by making intranets first to work out the kinks.

---

2   Brad Frost, "Design Systems Are for User Interfaces," November 15, 2021,
    https://bradfrost.com/blog/post/design-systems-are-for-user-interfaces/

Try to follow the textbook and make notes about where the textbook just isn't right.

That's the design system. Not the textbook. The design system is the notes in the margin. That's what's been contributed back: the stories, the solutions. The nice thing about doing this in the context of making digital products is that you don't have to settle for notes in the margin. You get to update the textbook itself. Every product used as a design system pilot makes the textbook more and more accurate so that it gets easier for everyone to do it the right way.

The Piloting Process

The process of piloting a design system is a cyclical one. Cycles and feedback loops are important ingredients in any system. These cycles are primary mechanisms for how a system self-corrects.

Within the practice of design systems, linking design system growth and product creation creates a virtuous cycle, a positive feedback loop that generates momentum (Figure 5.4). But how does an organization start the cycle? It's a classic chicken/egg problem. Is one place better to start than the other?

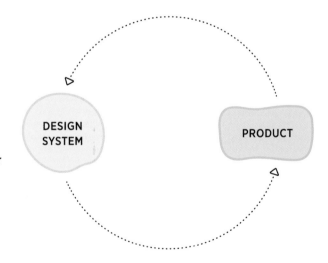

FIGURE 5.4
The virtuous cycle for digital organizations relies on building positive momentum between design system and product.

The answer is to start with product. Product comes before system. I prefer a slightly modified diagram that I call "the Measuring Spoon Cycle for Design Systems" (Figure 5.5). (Because it's shaped like a measuring spoon? See? I know; it needs work.) In short, this is the most successful process for making a design system that I've seen yet.

1. Make a feature or product.
2. Extract and abstract components from that feature or product to start the system.
3. Make another product using the components you previously extracted.
4. Return to Step 2.

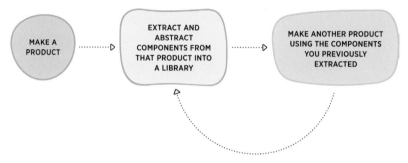

FIGURE 5.5
Kick-starting the virtuous cycle of a design system practice should start with product.

Then repeat this process. Forever. For as long as your company exists.

The nice thing about the Measuring Spoon Cycle is that it applies equally to a new team making their first product and system as much as it does to an organization that's had a design system for many years and wants to improve it. It's never too late to start—or restart—this flywheel.

Piloting a Design System from Scratch

Some organizations find themselves in a "blank slate" phase regarding design systems. It could be a startup making its first set of digital products. Or it could be an established organization that has so much interface sprawl or design/code debt that starting from scratch feels like a more viable path over untangling what already exists to build on top of. Whatever the case, here are some examples of how you can use a pilot process to identify some starting points for your design system.

Piloting Unity, ExxonMobil's Design System

When I worked with ExxonMobil in 2016 to help them create their design system, Unity, they had 500 developers and only one designer (hi Chris!). The biggest need from the outset was to figure out how to scale design inside the organization in a way that promoted brand consistency without it being enforced by any one person or team in particular. Developers were largely left to their own devices to build products. Some had design skills; others tried to use libraries like Bootstrap or Material Design that already had some design baked in by default. That meant there was a wide range of variance among all of the digital products created at ExxonMobil (Figure 5.6).

FIGURE 5.6
ExxonMobil apps sport a range of looks before a unified design system came along.

The team's work began by picking a few applications to use as pilots for the design system and talking to the designers and developers making those applications, as well as some of the users of those applications. We started to design and build the features and functionality that users needed from these applications. We didn't do anything too "design system-y," like defining a global color palette or writing principles or anything like that. Instead, we started to let that kind of work be emergent. We started with the Good Ol' Product Design Process.™

One of our pilots was their Agenda Creator product (Figure 5.7), a necessity for organizations that need to structure their many meetings. We did stakeholder research and customer research, just like you would in any good product design process. We learned what functionality needed to be there and didn't. We came up with a new design that was a bit simpler and more modern with a sharper focus on the primary customer needs (Figure 5.8).

FIGURE 5.7
ExxonMobil's Agenda Creator product before a design system was implemented.

FIGURE 5.8
ExxonMobil's new Agenda Creator product.

Once we were done designing and building this product, we looked at it again from the perspective of understanding what pieces could be abstracted and extracted for other ExxonMobil teams to use. The header in Figure 5.9 is a good example. By extracting the header from this Agenda Creator product, the next team to use it got the benefit of all the good thinking and hard work that went into making this header in the first place. It's responsive. It has all the right typefaces and brand attributes within it. It's been tested for accessibility and for performance. The behavior has been QA'd. It's pulled straight out of a product and ready for others to use where applicable.

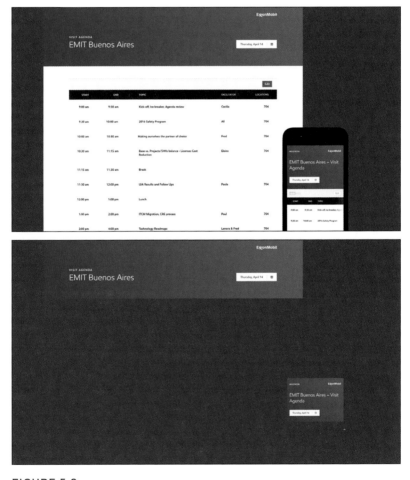

FIGURE 5.9
The Agenda Creator header is a perfect design system candidate because other teams could use it right away.

This isn't a perfect header or a header that every team could use in perpetuity. It doesn't even have navigation in it! But it didn't need to. This team needed a header without navigation—which we found out through the product design process research activities—so there's a high likelihood that maybe another team might need one, too.

Notice that what we didn't do was start abstractly. We didn't say, "Let's make a header that everyone can use." If we had started that way, we probably would have overdesigned and overengineered the header. We probably would have tried to plan for any type of header that could exist whether it had mega drop-downs and search boxes and global nav and utility nav and all sorts of stuff in it that we had no idea would be used, rather than working from a very particular use case. It's the other way around: let's build a product and extract its header into a design system for anyone who might make use of it. Pilots give components context that you wouldn't have otherwise.

Agenda Creator was the first pilot. The second pilot was the Identity & Access Management Portal (Figure 5.10).

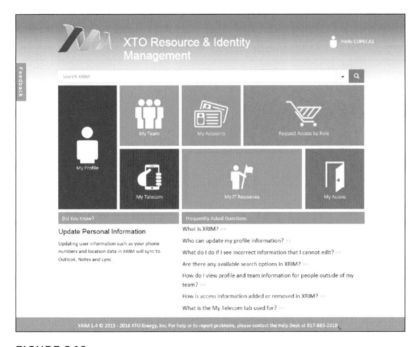

FIGURE 5.10

ExxonMobil's Identity & Access Management Portal product before a design system was implemented.

We realized we could use the header we extracted from Agenda Creator, although it needed a few tweaks. So, we tweaked it for the new design (Figure 5.11). We added a few more pieces like navigation links and a search bar.

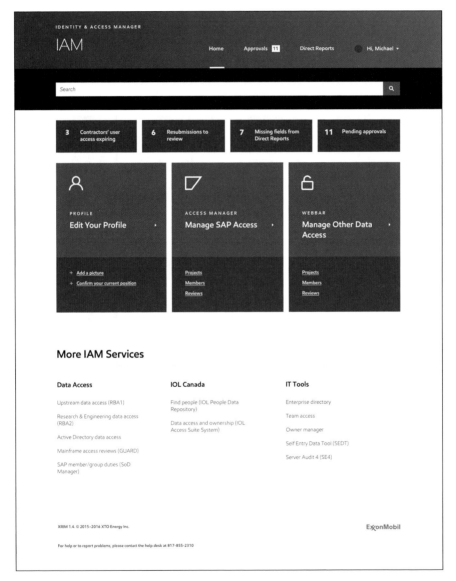

FIGURE 5.11
ExxonMobil's new Identity & Access Manager product.

What I hope you can anticipate is that, after working on five or six different pilots, we had a few variations of our header (Figure 5.12) with things like drop-down menus and utility links and mega navs, and also versions that didn't have those elements when they weren't necessary. Sometimes it's just a logo and a title and a navigation. Each of these variations was easy to create because it came from specific product requirements and a previously tested version. Since we had a few robust header variations, we should never have to create a header from scratch again. We would likely tweak it with more variations, but most of the heavy lifting should be done.

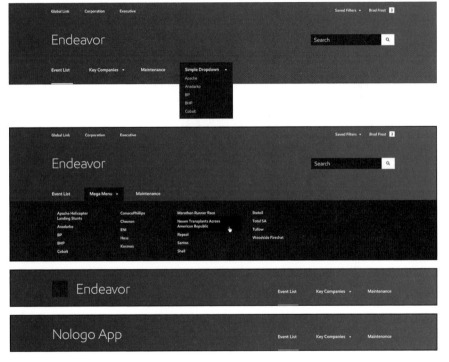

FIGURE 5.12
Different variations of the header in Unity.

Now that we had all these headers, it made sense to put them somewhere with helpful instructions so that other teams could easily find and use them. That's the purpose of a design system reference site, and this is the exact part of the process—the point where you have a component extracted from a product that doesn't yet have a home—where you add it to that reference site. Figure 5.13 shows a page of headers and footers that we got from extracting them from real products for Unity, ExxonMobil's design system.

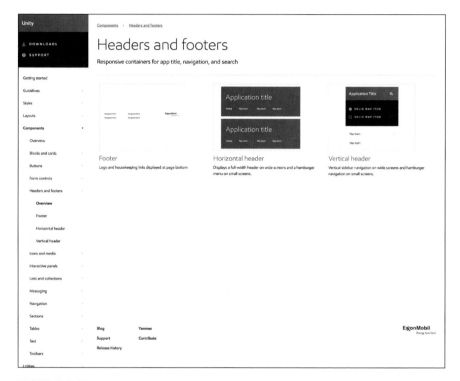

FIGURE 5.13

This is the time in the piloting process to add all variations of a component to a page in a reference site.

The header component detail page (Figure 5.14) has so much useful information about the header, such as different variations, code to implement, usage guidelines like do's and don'ts, class name and API documentation, and much more. After doing a lot of pilots, you get a really robust reference site as a by-product of the product design process.

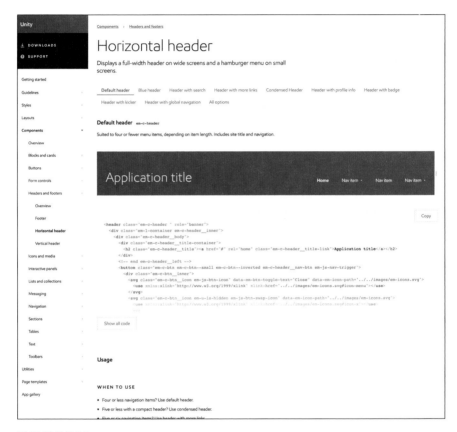

FIGURE 5.14

The header component detail page shows all the info someone needs to know how to use it.

Piloting Seton Hill University's Web Presence

In 2015, I helped create a design system for a Catholic liberal arts university just outside of Pittsburgh, Pennsylvania, called Seton Hill University. As with the ExxonMobil example, creating that design system started with the regular Good Ol' Product Design Process.™

On the "Areas of Study" template (Figure 5.15), there's a component halfway down the page with a label of "From Degrees to Careers." The idea was that we could show the kinds of jobs that students with this degree typically got after graduating. We designed it, and we built it. We fittingly called it the "From Degrees to Careers" component. We figured it would be a one-off component (sometimes called a *snowflake*, as we didn't think it would be very reusable.

We made a few more pages, like Campus Life (Figure 5.16). Our research strongly suggested that a calendar of events on campus would be really useful to students, so our team discussed how to add it to the Campus Life page in the best possible way. We realized we could use a pretty similar format to the "From Degrees to Careers" component, so we mocked up a variation of it for this page.

From an implementation and code standpoint, it felt a little bit odd to use something called the "From Degrees to Careers" component for upcoming events. So, we had a few choices here:

1. We could duplicate the "From Degrees to Careers" component and make a similar "Upcoming Events" component, but it felt a little weird to have two separate components that were basically the same thing.

2. We could abstract the "From Degrees to Careers" component to serve both use cases.

We went with the second option (as you probably would have done). We abstracted it into a component called the "Vertical Tabs" component (Figure 5.17). That way, it could be a flexible user interface that could accept many different kinds of content and have a few variations on how it might be styled.

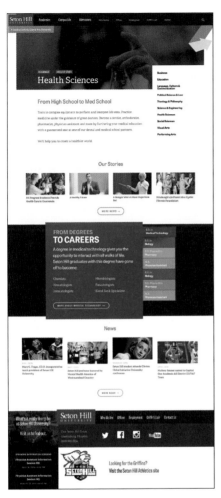

FIGURE 5.15
The "From Degrees to Careers" component is a unique area of the page.

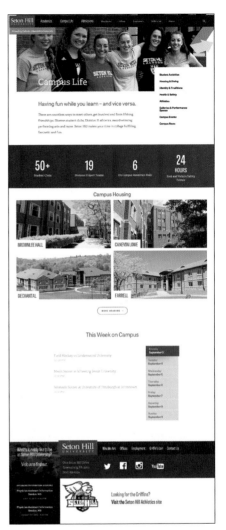

FIGURE 5.16
The "Upcoming Events" component looks strangely familiar to the "From Degrees to Careers" component.

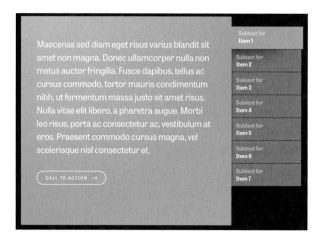

FIGURE 5.17
An abstracted Vertical Tabs component can work for both the "From Degrees to Careers" content as well as the "Upcoming Events" content.

Whenever I share this kind of example, I usually get two specific kinds of reactions.

The first reaction is, "Isn't this backward? Couldn't you have started by making a Vertical Tabs component and then using it on each one of these pages?" The answer is yes, I could have done that, but I didn't know I needed it until I started designing these pages. It's significantly easier to fill your design system with components you actually need and will use when you have real content and real use cases. Many organizations have a design system graveyard full of components no one really needs right now that also doesn't have components that everybody actually *does* need right now.

The second reaction I get is often framed as a criticism: "You took something cool and made it boring." Yes! Thank you for noticing! That's the point of design systems. As UX design leader Josh Clark says in his article, "The Most Exciting Design Systems Are Boring," "Design systems are containers for institutional knowledge. Identify the design problems teams confront over and over again. The more common the problem the better. Design systems should prioritize the mundane."[3] If you look at the stuff that a design system consists of that comes out of the piloting process, it's all the boring stuff, the elements you don't ever want to be making over and over again: paragraphs, check boxes, radio buttons, alerts buttons. It's not about reinventing the wheel; it's about mass producing the wheel so more people can more easily experience their own adventures.

---

3   Josh Clark, "The Most Exciting Design Systems Are Boring," April 3, 2017, https://bigmedium.com/ideas/boring-design-systems.html.

If you work on any kind of digital business, thinking and building in terms of patterns is incredibly valuable for your organization, as it will help you build leaner, faster, and more future-friendly. One of the most important lessons I've learned in creating modular design systems is that there's a difference between *content components* and *display components*:

- A *content component* describes the types of elements within and can be rendered in multiple forms.

- A *display component* describes a specific rendering and can be applied to multiple types of content components.

What does that mean?! Let's look at a common example. When constructing a page, I'll often hear a team member say something like, "We can use the event component here." What does that actually mean? Perhaps the most obvious place to start is from a previously designed comp that looks like Figure 5.18.

FIGURE 5.18
A simple event component with a title, date, and location.

A simple way to mark that up could look like this:

```
<div class="event">
  <h1 class="event__title">Star Wars: The Force Awakens Premiere</h1>
  <p class="event__date">Dec 20, 2015</p>
  <p class="event__location">Ritz East, Philadelphia PA</p>
</div>
```

While there's nothing technically incorrect about this markup, it may not be abstract enough for reuse. As you think about the content model for an event, the pieces displayed here are:

- Title
- Date
- Location

continues

There's nothing that ties an event to this specific display. Other types of content that may exist on the site could have similar content models, like articles: title, date, description. I could easily use the same display component to render an article (Figure 5.19).

FIGURE 5.19

A simple Article component with a title, publish date, and description.

Interaction designer Alla Kholmatova wisely observed,[4] "If you give [a component] a presentational name, its future will be limited, because it will be confined by its style." Calling this an event component might mean that I never even consider it for an article, even though it could work just as well.

So, how can you make a more useful component? Abstract the display from both an event as well as an article into a component that can apply to both (Figure 5.20).

FIGURE 5.20

A more abstracted component that can work for both events and articles.

4   Alla Kholmatova," Design Systems," *Smashing Magazine* AG, 2017.

With an abstracted display component like this, you can choose multiple kinds of content patterns (events, articles, etc.) to visualize. That leads to an interesting approach when thinking about how to think and talk about components in design systems:

1. Identify the type of content (content component).

2. Choose a visual option (display component) to render said content.

What does this look like in practice? On a previous project we'd worked on together, my team decided that wireframes were too time-consuming to make and constrained our client's thinking on graphic design a little too much. We realized that the most valuable thing about our previous wireframes was having a list of content for each page. So, when our information architect sat down to map out the content strategy for the site, she whipped out a list of components for each major page on the site (Figure 5.21).

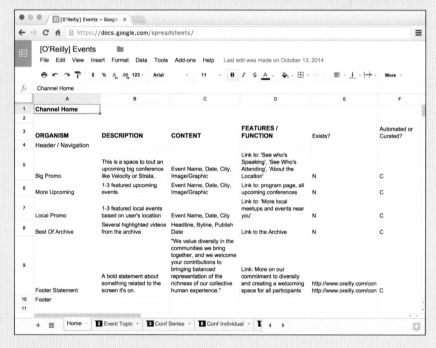

FIGURE 5.21

Content descriptions without visual suggestions allow everyone to work with ideal versions of content and user interface elements.

continues

This allowed the engineer and me to work simultaneously, assembling all the parts in our own ways and riffing off each other's work. Seeing this process unfold revealed another important insight: when working, content strategists primarily think about content components, designers primarily think about display components, and front-end engineers are responsible for bringing the two together. Certainly, a bit of an oversimplification, but I've witnessed it being true more often than not. It's obvious in hindsight but easily overlooked when you're heads-down in the middle of a project.

Look at that spreadsheet. "Big Promo," "More Upcoming," and "Local Promo" are all listed as separate components because they do different jobs (see the "Features/Functions" column), but their content components are exactly the same. Our information architect made sure that the engineer and I wouldn't forget about that content and left it up to me to decide on the best display components for this data to be rendered across different screen sizes. The engineer and I could decide how much to abstract these in code to make them as reusable and easily understood as possible.

I hypothesized that we could build these content components with multiple instances of just two display components, so I started by designing these (see Figure 5.22).

The engineer then translated both display components into one block of code:

```
<div class="g-item">
  <div class="block block-thumb">
    <div class="b-thumb">...</div>
    <div class="b-text">
      <h2 class="b-title">...</h2>
      <div class="date-city">...</div>
      <div class="dek">...</div>
    </div>
    <!-- .b-text -->
  </div>
  <!-- .block -->
</div>
<!-- .g-item -->
```

Large

KICKER

Title of Event
Date, Location

Description text aenean lacinia bibendum nulla sed consectetur. Fusce dapibus, tellus ac cursus commodo, tortor mauris condimentum nibh, ut fermentum massa.

Small

KICKER

Title of Event
Date, Location

Description text aenean lacinia bibendum nulla sed consectetur. Fusce dapibus, tellus ac cursus commodo, tortor mauris condimentum nibh, ut fermentum massa.

FIGURE 5.22

Abstracted variations of display components that can work for anything with a title, description, metadata, image, and kicker.

continues

He then created a modifier called `.g-item-hero` that turns the small display component into the large one.

The final page ended up looking something like Figure 5.23.

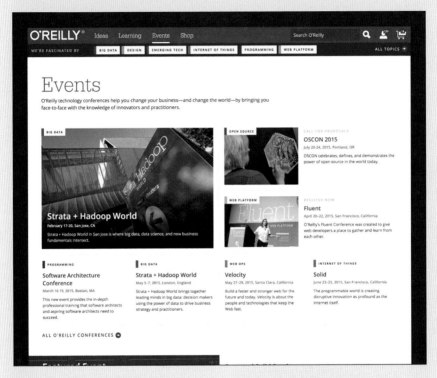

FIGURE 5.23
Content descriptions without visual suggestions allow everyone to work with ideal versions of content and user interface elements.

In short: three sections powered by one display component—which we ended up calling a "media object"—with two different views based on size, written as one code block with one modifier.

As general guidelines, don't let your display components describe the content within and don't let your content components suggest anything about their presentation. With a construct like this, each person's job could break down like this. Initially:

- The content strategist's job would be to define the content components.
- The designer's job would be to create display components.
- The engineer's job would be to create the markup for the display component and create the hooks for content to flow into the display components appropriately.

Where this all becomes really liberating and powerful is when you can have an army of display components that can work with an infinite amount of content components. Distinctions like these become incredibly useful in how you can work on component-based modular designs.

Piloting a Design System from Existing Products

One of the most prevalent design system challenges today is when a person or a small team receives the charge to start a design system at an organization that already has more than a handful of digital websites and applications that end users use. How do you pilot a design system when there are already plenty of existing products to choose from?

Collecting the Best and Best Practices

Many design system teams start their design system journey with an interface inventory,[5] an exercise to collect the many different existing user interface elements to look for patterns and commonalities. These teams often use the output of the inventory to demonstrate the amount of unintentional variation to the wider organization. In other words, "Look at all this redundancy and inefficiency!"

But an oft-missed opportunity from this exercise is to collect the good stuff along with the bad. In fact, overlooking this responsibility is one of the biggest missteps and misconceptions design teams have of themselves.

Many see their role on a design system team as an opportunity to create best practices that the rest of the organization can then employ. "I'll design one button to rule them all," the naïve design system designer thinks. But creating something new and convincing everyone else to use it is nontrivial. In fact, it's one of the primary hurdles to widespread design system adoption. Instead, the primary job of a design system team is to collect the organization's best practices and prepare them for scaling. Highlight what's already been done in the past that works. In his book *Do Scale*,[6] advisor Les McKeown summarizes, "Scalability is built on mastering the mundane."

One way to reflect on whether your team is mastering the mundane is to reflect on your language. Scrutinize your job descriptions, Kanban boards, and conversations you have about your work. If you're constantly using words like *create*, *generate*, or *define*, your team might have too much of a propensity to see themselves as the authority than they should, and you're probably in for an uphill journey

---

5   Brad Frost, "Interface Inventory," July 10, 2013, **https://bradfrost.com/blog/post/interface-inventory/**

6   Les McKeown, *Do Scale*. (London, England: The Do Book Co., 2019).

in adoption. But if your team tends to gravitate toward words like *collect*, *curate*, and *establish* as their foremost roles, that spirit will serve you well and lay out a smoother path for others to want to use and contribute to your design system.

Once you've adopted a collector mindset, start collecting your organization's best stuff, which begs the question: what constitutes "best?" Here are a few simple ways you might define "best" (see Table 5.2).

TABLE 5.2   DEFINING "BEST" AT YOUR ORGANIZATION

Organizational Priority	Definition of "Best"
Performance	Fastest loading components
Customer satisfaction	Components on pages with least customer complaints
Technical powers	Well-coded components
Aesthetic	Components with beautiful user interface

In Chapter 3, "The Parts of a Design System Product," I mentioned connectedness as an important criterion for a true design system. That doesn't just apply on the technology side. Connecting design system goals and activities to larger and broader organizational priorities ensures that design systems efforts aren't isolated or treated as secondary. The more you infuse the design system with the regular and vital goings-on of the rest of the organization, the more wins you'll experience there, too.

Collecting as an Exercise of Inclusion

You can also use your definition of "best" to signal important values about your design system, in particular how inclusive you intend the system to be.

For example, you can choose to include in your design system some components that teams are really proud of making, signaling that the design system is a place that spotlights teams' accomplishments.

I once worked with an organization that had a component everyone knew as "Fred." Every feature team had an instance of Fred within their work, even before an official design system team was established. When it came time to make a design system, Fred was obviously the first official contribution. Because the organization already had an affinity for Fred, including Fred in the design system brought along some of that affinity with it. When fondness exists at a local (read: feature or product) level, collecting and promoting it to a deeper and more connected level of importance with a design system is a great way to get people to want to use the design system, because they recognize something they're already drawn to.

You can also use the exercise of collecting to make friends around your organization. Perhaps there's a team that tends to want to do their own thing. Or maybe there's a team that everyone seems to stay away from. Including a component or pattern they've made in a newly established design system signals that you want them to be part of the shared foundation. It's a way to say, "We want you to be part of this initiative, because you're already a part of it," and that signal is a major driver of adoption for design systems.

The IKEA effect is a cognitive bias coined in 2012 by researchers Michael Norton, Daniel Mochon, and Dan Ariely that says people place disproportionately higher value on items they had a hand in creating. It taps into the psychological need to feel competent and that your work was worth it. The IKEA effect is a big reason that designers and engineers will either try to create a new system on their own or prefer their own highly modified versions of systems like Google's Material Design or (formerly) Twitter's Bootstrap. You can combat that cognitive bias with your design system by signaling, "Hey, you've made this thing, too" and proving it by including elements that others have created, not just the design system team.

Piloting a Speculative Nike Design System

As an example, let's examine a brand like Nike that has many different public websites and applications in the wild to demonstrate how to extract a design system from existing digital products.

First up: taking inventory. Might they already have a design system in use?

Let's start with the flagship website, Nike.com (Figure 5.24). There are many components you'd expect to find on a flagship website: navigation, logo, headers, buttons, hero elements, various typographic styles, product cards, calls to action, and more.

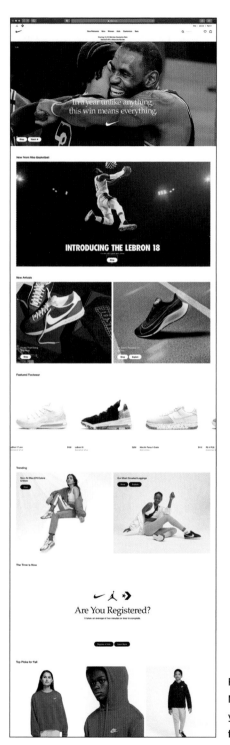

FIGURE 5.24
Nike.com has many elements you'd expect to find on a flagship ecommerce website.

Next up: Nike's news site (Figure 5.25). It contains many of the same visual elements from the .com, but there is a decent amount of small variance. For those of you who are typographically minded, you may have already noticed that there's a slight difference in typefaces here from what we saw on the flagship website. This site uses the sans serif typeface Circular for headlines, which didn't appear on the .com.

Also, while the header looks somewhat consistent, all of the navigation items are now hidden under an icon with three vertical lines, lovingly referred to as a "hamburger menu icon."

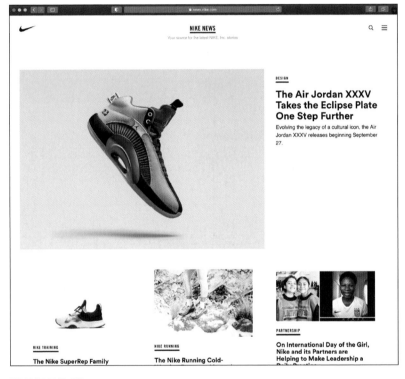

FIGURE 5.25
The Nike News site kinda feels like a Nike site, but there is some variance from Nike.com.

Continuing over to the Purpose site (Figure 5.26), there's more variance here, too. The navigation is back and exposed; it's no longer under a hamburger menu icon. But now, there's some variation in the typography, as it's using a much bolder condensed sans serif (Futura) to pair with sans serif body copy (Helvetica Neue) and a serif (Palatino) for additional flavor. And from a components and aesthetic point of view, there are much splashier hero elements with illustration and video on this site than the previous ones.

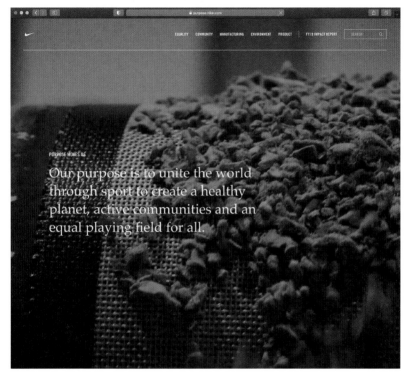

FIGURE 5.26
The Nike Purpose site kinda feels like a Nike site, but there is some variance from Nike.com.

Moving on to the Jobs site (Figure 5.27), there is even more variance. The header looks close to the previous examples, but with different typography and sizing. The interaction on the page is very animation-heavy, driven by scrolling.

FIGURE 5.27

The Nike Jobs site kinda feels like a Nike site, but there is some variance from Nike.com.

Over to the Investors site (Figure 5.28), the Trade Gothic sans-serif is back but in more of a leading role. There is also more of a beveled Web 2.0 look in the header where there is some dimension rather than that flat design look that was on the previous sites.

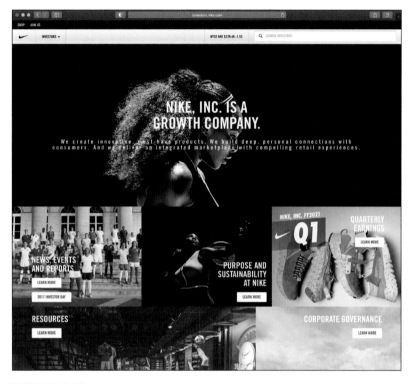

FIGURE 5.28

The Nike Investors site kinda feels like a Nike site, but there is some variance from Nike.com.

Let's look at some native applications, too. Although visually similar, the Nike Shopping app (Figure 5.29) has many more components designed for interaction like tab sets, carousels, and accordions, as opposed to the mobile site which has many more static calls to action (Figure 5.30).

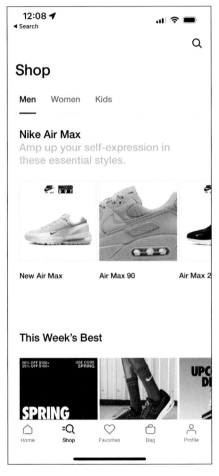

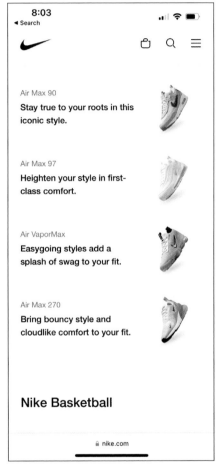

FIGURE 5.29
The Nike shopping native mobile app.

FIGURE 5.30
The Nike shopping mobile website.

The SNKRS app (Figure 5.31) uses similar conventions as the Nike Shopping app, but there are small variations in what could be identical elements like tabs or icons.

Looking at these sites and apps in aggregate (Figure 5.32), it's easy to notice the little differences in variation. Big differences are easy to justify, because different content often needs different ways to be expressed, but it's all the little stuff that exposes the lack of a system.

If you solely look at just all the headers here (Figure 5.33), look how closely they're related, but not quite the same. Why are these different? This kind of variation is much more difficult to justify and often doesn't have a good explanation. It exposes that each of these things was probably designed and built individually without the qualities of what a system should actually contain. It's the small inconsistencies, not the big ones.

FIGURE 5.31
The Nike SNKRS native mobile app.

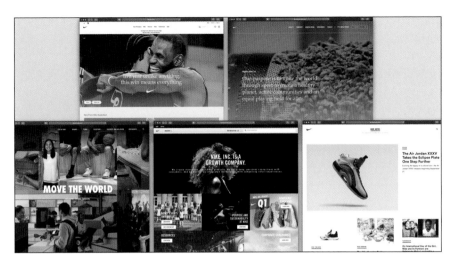

FIGURE 5.32
Comparing Nike websites to search for common patterns.

FIGURE 5.33
Comparing headers reveals inconsistencies. Intentional or not?

Looking under the hood at the code side, too, the inconsistency is even more apparent (Figure 5.34). For navigation front-end code across three sites, one has a class name of `pre-l-nav`, another has a class name of `nav-main`, and the third has a class of `main-menu`, even though it looks like all three have very similar styling and behavior. Again, this kind of small variation exposes the fact that this was probably created without some of the other versions in mind or without anyone who had an overview and an oversight of all of these things. In short, because these sites are connected where they could and should be, it's a safe assumption that no shared system was used and may not even exist.

FIGURE 5.34
Comparing code that could be the same but isn't.

Minimum Viable Design System

If our assumptions are correct that there isn't an existing design system, it's time to make one! You've just done the inventorying; now it's time to collect the best stuff. Trying to collect three best components and practices is a great place to start. The driving question you should try to answer is, "What three components could other teams use right now?" Through inventorying and talking to teams, you decide that these three elements are worthwhile candidates (Figure 5.35):

- **Account Bar:** Its vertical format and limited horizontal space is the least visually disruptive to existing sites when implemented.
- **Button:** Everyone seems to be trending toward using this one anyway.
- **Nav Drop-down:** It's a great example of balancing brand and functionality.

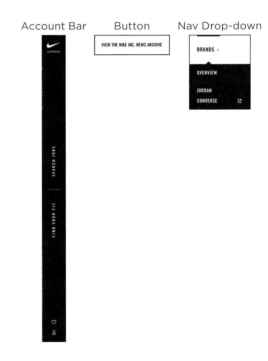

FIGURE 5.35
Here are the three elements to begin a design system.

These three elements are the beginning of a Nike design system! You might be surprised to hear that just three elements can be a design system. After all, most of the popular design systems out there feature dozens if not hundreds of components, so how could three components be sufficient?

Remember that the design system definition from Chapter 1, "Why Design Systems?," proposed that a design system was the *smallest* set of components that could be useful. Many teams view design systems as an all-or-nothing proposition, that an app has to be fully composed of design system components to realize value. This is simply false. If even one component from a design system saves a feature team a week, a few days, or even a few hours of time, the design system is already proving its value. I'll share more about appropriate targets and goals for design system usage, adoption, and coverage in Chapter 9, "Success Metrics for a Design System."

Design Systems Are Emergent

In 1987, business management consultant Henry Mintzberg wrote an article for *Harvard Business Review* called, "Crafting Strategy,"[7] and it could not be more appropriate to design system work. Mintzberg wrote, "Strategies that appear without clear intentions—or in spite of them—[are called] emergent strategies. Actions simply converge into patterns...deliberate strategy precludes learning once the strategy is formulated; emergent strategy fosters it. People take actions one by one and respond to them, so that patterns eventually form."

More often than not, the practice of design systems is one of emergent strategy. Creating a design system in a vacuum and then trying to plug it into an organization's rapidly moving product design process rarely works. Piloting works because it allows patterns to emerge organically over time in a way that reflects the reality of an organization and rolls with its natural pace.

When you look at a list of basic components that exist in a design system (Figure 5.36), it's easy to assume that it's a list of prerequisites, like all the ingredients before you bake a cake. But that's only because there's no context to the list. It's the wrong metaphor.

---

7 Henry Mintzberg, "Crafting Strategy," July 1987, **https://hbr.org/1987/07/crafting-strategy**

FIGURE 5.36
Are these jars of ingredients to make dishes or storage after dishes have
been made? It's impossible to tell just by looking at them.

Imagine instead that you inherited an antique car from a relative. While the car was a beautiful and exquisite piece of machinery in its heyday, years of sitting around have concealed its luster, and it just doesn't drive anymore.

So, you decide to restore it. You carefully disassemble the car so you can clean it; tune the parts that can still work after some love; and replace some parts that just don't work anymore for brand new ones. At some point, you end up with all the parts disassembled on your garage floor.

That's what this list is. Rather than thinking of this as a list of inputs, instead consider this the list of outputs from the piloting process. You've taken apart a product team's application or website. And before you create a new digital product, you have a bunch of parts on the garage floor, ready and waiting to be reassembled into something new. It's what comes out of the product design process that then can go into the design system. It's not the first step that starts the Measuring Spoon Cycle. It's a natural part of already being in the cycle. This list reflects a moment in time, just after something has been deconstructed and just before you'll use the parts to make something new and even better.

Extracting and Abstracting

I've written about "extracting and abstracting" components a lot in this chapter, but how exactly does one extract and abstract a component? What does that mean? What does that look like in a literal sense?

As you're scrutinizing your organization's many digital products, you're bound to encounter multiple variations of the same component, likely stemming from the lack of connection between design teams. For example, a cursory glance through multiple digital products from an American insurance company, Allstate, reveals nine separate kinds of text inputs (Figure 5.37).

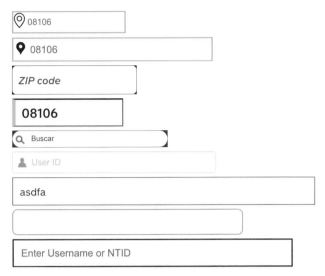

FIGURE 5.37
Different text inputs for the same brand.

How could you reconcile all of these into one canonical version? The big risk here is that you ultimately end up creating the 10th version instead of a canonical version, reminiscent of the famous xkcd comic on standards (Figure 5.38).

FIGURE 5.38
Design system work often toes the fine line of creating yet another competing standard.

HOW STANDARDS PROLIFERATE:
(SEE: A/C CHARGERS, CHARACTER ENCODINGS, INSTANT MESSAGING, ETC)

SITUATION: THERE ARE 14 COMPETING STANDARDS.

14?! RIDICULOUS! WE NEED TO DEVELOP ONE UNIVERSAL STANDARD THAT COVERS EVERYONE'S USE CASES. YEAH!

SOON:

SITUATION: THERE ARE 15 COMPETING STANDARDS.

XKCD. "STANDARDS." HTTPS://XKCD.COM/927/

The key lies in reusing as much of what already exists within each of these variations. Note the commonalities across four different criteria (Table 5.3).

TABLE 5.3   IDENTIFYING COMPONENT CRITERIA

All	What does every version of this component have in common?
Most	What do most versions of this component have in common?
Some	What do some versions of this component have in common?
Few	What do few versions of this component have in common?

In the case of this text input component, the chart breaks down like so (Table 5.4):

TABLE 5.4   FILLING IN COMPONENT CRITERIA

All	White background Border
Most	Placeholder text
Some	Rounded shape vs. rectangular shape Italic placeholder text vs. regular placeholder text Border vs. no border
Few	Icon

As you start to design and build the "new" abstracted component, approach each area of the chart with these directives (Table 5.5):

TABLE 5.5   A RUBRIC FOR ABSTRACTING A COMPONENT

All	Every characteristic is mandatory.
Most	Every characteristic is highly recommended.
Some	Prepare proposals and/or facilitate workshop to form consensus.
Few	Delay including these characteristics.

All and *Few* are the simplest. If every text input has a white background, make sure that the consolidated, abstracted component has a white background. If only a few text inputs have icons, don't include an icon just yet; wait for that obligation to become more common.

Most is a little trickier, but not much. If most text inputs have placeholder text, it's a safe enough bet that your abstracted component should have placeholder text.

Some is the most contentious criteria by far. If some text inputs are rounded and others are rectangular, how do you resolve that conflict? The most infallible way is to facilitate a workshop. Call together as many people who have their own versions of the text input as possible and get them to agree to as much as you can. This effectively moves the characteristics up into the *All* or *Most* categories. For characteristics where an agreement can't be reached, try to at least get the participants to agree that the design system team's choice will be the tiebreaker.

Given all of this, your abstracted text component may end up looking something like Figure 5.39.

FIGURE 5.39
A consolidated text component from nine separate sources.

The important thing about this version is that as many people as possible can look at it and conclude, "That looks pretty close to what we already have," because they recognize some overlapping characteristics. In that way, they may feel like they've "contributed" that characteristic, which is a major boon for component adoption.

Questions for Reflection

- Given where your organization is right now, would it be more fruitful to pilot a design system from scratch or from existing products?
- What are the "best" pieces of digital interfaces happening at your organization right now?
- Complete a pilot scorecard for your organization's roadmap. What do the scores tell you about how to best grow a design system at your organization? How close is it to your current roadmap sequence?
- What three components could make up your "minimal viable design system?"

CHAPTER 6

Governance and Contribution

Far and away, the conversations most teams I work with want to have are on the topics of design system contribution and governance. That's usually because these are the places they see the most resistance: they see very little contribution, and, even when contribution does happen, it's not in the way the design system team wants.

In her book, *Managing Chaos: Digital Governance by Design* (Rosenfeld Media cross-sell achievement unlocked!), management consultant Lisa Welchman emphasizes the importance of digital governance: it clarifies roles and responsibilities for collaborative teams. I've seen two common scenarios where design system governance goes wrong:

- Teams define the right roles and the responsibilities but link them incorrectly.
- Teams understand the theory, but often get lost in the application of the specifics.

To address both of these common pitfalls, let's turn to a long-established model for framing: the world of open source.

The WordPress Ecosystem as It Relates to Design Systems

WordPress is a free, open-source content management system that powers 43% of the top 10 million websites. It was released in 2003 and still remains heavily in use almost 20 years later.

Part of the reason for WordPress's longevity and scale is the way it's maintained. Consider the different kinds of groups involved in the ecosystem of WordPress:

- The WordPress core team consists of 5–10 developers, including co-founder Matt Mullenweg.
- Automattic is the company behind WordPress (among other ventures) that employs around 2,000 people, some of whom get paid to work on WordPress full-time.
- As of July 2023, there have been 56,326 contributions to WordPress Core.[1]

---

1 "Make WordPress Core," Automattic, July 31, 2023, **https://core.trac.wordpress.org/changeset**

- WordPress has a number of contributors who get paid by their own companies (not Automattic) to work on WordPress, because it is a crucial tool to their business. Automattic employee Chuck Grimmett estimates that around 523 people on average have contributed to each version of WordPress from 5.0–6.0 that don't work at Automattic.[2]

- WordPress has millions of users who conceivably have never and will never contribute to it. It's estimated that 43% of the top 10 million websites use WordPress, and even with a conservative estimate of one WordPress developer for each of those sites, that's a base of 4.3 million users.

In short, and with the most generous interpretation of the data:

- Only 0.05% of WordPress users get paid to work on it.
- Only 0.01% of WordPress users contribute back to it.
- Only 0.0002% of WordPress users are directly responsible for it.

That should set some expectations for what you might see and what's realistic for your organization's design system. Many design system teams expect every team that uses the design system to contribute back to it, which is just unrealistic.

Having been around for as long as it has, WordPress certainly benefits from the economies of scale that you won't have early on, so here's a little fudge factor translation for how this may relate to your organization's design system. If 100 people in your organization use your design system:

- About 2 people (2%) should be expected to contribute back.
- About 6 people (6%) should be paid to work on it full-time or mostly full-time.
- 1 (1%) person should be directly responsible for it (likely the design system product owner).

(I'll share more about these roles in Chapter 7, "Roles and Responsibilities.")

This gives you some benchmarks for what to expect within your design system ecosystem.

---

2   Chuck Grimmett, "Some WordPress Core Contributor Stats," September 24, 2022, https://cagrimmett.com/data-viz/2022/09/24/some-wp-core-contributor-stats/

A Framework for Design System Governance

Here is a framework of the primary questions to answer regarding design system governance in this order:

1. What are the design system activities that need to be done?
2. Why should these design system activities be done?
3. Who should do these design system activities?
4. When should these design system activities be done?
5. Where and how should these design system activities be done?

Fortunately, many others have written extensively about the subject of design system governance. Let's examine all of the pieces.

What Are the Design System Activities That Need to Be Done?

In Getting Vanilla ready for v1: the roadmap,[3] design producer Inayaili de León lays out a flowchart to define the process for adding new patterns and components to a design system (Figure 6.1). Each organization's design system workflow may be slightly different due to internal processes and culture, but the general questions to be answered in a workflow document are shared:

- When do I use the system and when do I make something on my own?
- How does something new make its way back into the system?

Whatever steps you include, make sure that it fits seamlessly within the current process of product design your company uses (Figure 6.2). Don't just start and end your flowchart with design system tasks. The beginning of this workflow should be a step that's already in your product design workflow, and the last step of this workflow is to transition back into that existing product design workflow.

---

3   Inayaili de León, "Getting Vanilla Ready for v1: The Roadmap," July 8, 2016, https://medium.com/@yaili/getting-vanilla-ready-for-v1-the-roadmap-8c0f4433f2f8

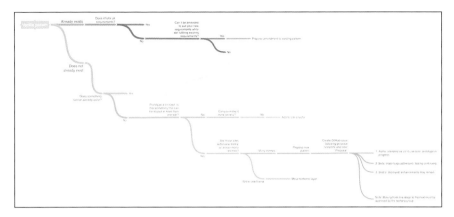

FIGURE 6.1

Inayaili de León's flowchart for adding a new component to the Vanilla design system at Canonical.

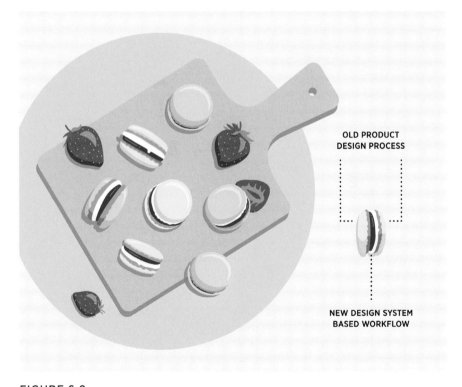

FIGURE 6.2

A new design system–based workflow is the perfect filling for your existing process.

Why Should These Design System Activities Be Done?

Because you're reading this book and have gotten this far, I'll assume you know why all of these design system activities are important: because life and work have way more to offer than wasting your days making the same data table from scratch over and over again. 'Nuff said.

Who Should Do Which Design System Activities?

In his article "Team Models for Scaling a Design System,"[4] design system consultant Nathan Curtis lays out the most common scenarios for how design system support teams are structured, with a soft recommendation for a federated model (Figure 6.3) that includes a subset of both centralized members and representative members of different products and features.

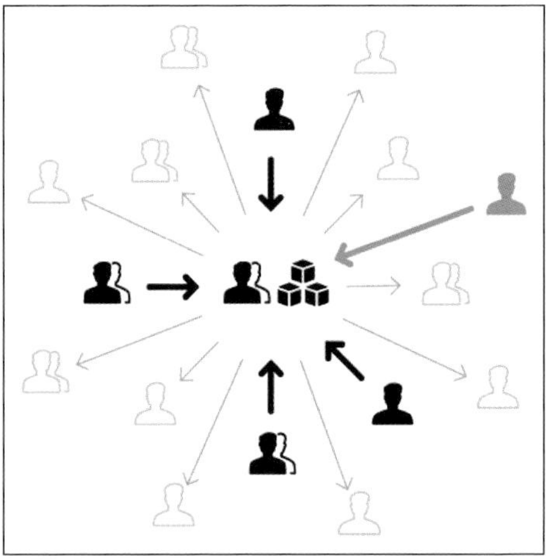

FIGURE 6.3
Nathan Curtis suggests a federated model of a representative group from around the organization to grow and evolve a design system.

Jina Anne—founder of design system conference Clarity—expands on that[5] in talking about her time at Salesforce, working on the

---

4   Nathan Curtis, "Team Models for Scaling a Design System," September 17, 2015, https://medium.com/eightshapes-llc/team-models-for-scaling-a-design-system-2cf9d03be6a0

5   Jina Anne, "The Salesforce Team Model for Scaling a Design System," October 13, 2015, https://medium.com/salesforce-ux/the-salesforce-team-model-for-scaling-a-design-system-d89c2a2d404b

Lightning Design System. She recommends a cyclical model (Figure 6.4), one where product teams and the design system team work together to create the virtuous cycle I mentioned in Chapter 5, "Pilots—The Best Way to Start and Sustain a Design System," where the design system informs product design and product design informs the design system.

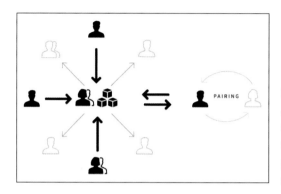

FIGURE 6.4
Jina Anne describes a cyclical model of responsibility between product teams and design system teams.

Having the wrong people doing the wrong work inside a design system ecosystem is probably the biggest source of unadopted design systems I've come across. This role confusion is directly tied to the poor "make system, use system" strategy I described in Chapter 4, "The Broken Business of 'Buy-In'." Perhaps the biggest value of thinking about design system work as a practice of emergent strategy is how it frames the idea of design system contribution, one of the most important and elusive steps in an organization's virtuous cycle of product design.

Why is contribution so tricky? For organizations that don't treat design system work as emergent, design system work and the product design cycle are often completely separate efforts. In that kind of organizational model, design system teams make components, product teams work on features, and it's no one's job in particular to figure out how the two fit together, and yet it's still somehow an expectation.

When you pilot, though, the roles of each team become much clearer. The job of the product and feature teams is to create valuable things for their customers: end users of their products. The job of the design system team is to collect the components and patterns the product teams are creating by extracting them from the product and abstracting them for other teams to use.

Said differently, it's the job of the design system team to contribute to the design system; it's not the product team's job. That's where most organizations get it wrong. They think the design system team's job is to create best practices and the job of the product teams is to somehow absorb and utilize those best practices and then magically figure out how to contribute to that set of best practices. I've seen design system teams create elaborate checklists that product teams need to comply with in order to contribute, and then they wonder why contribution is so low or even nonexistent. Contribution is difficult when the wrong people are responsible for it and when the systems in place—sprint plans, product velocity, a "move fast and break things" culture—disincentivize it. A better way is to let teams do what's easy, natural, familiar, and (hopefully) fun for them for as long as possible. Systems people want to do system things. Product people want to create things. This is the way.

I love to cook, but I don't do it often, because I make a gigantic mess when I cook. I'm all for cleaning my stations as I go, but there's still a bunch of cutting boards and knives and ramekins and plates that need washing and cleaning afterward. To avoid the work I don't want to do, I sacrifice the thing that I actually do want to do.

Luckily, we've struck a balance in our house. My wife Emily doesn't like cooking, but she doesn't mind cleaning at all. And she's great at it! She's way faster and better than I am at it with what looks to me like so much less effort than I generally have to exert when I clean.

So, we have an agreement: I cook, she cleans. We both (along with our kids) get a delicious meal, and we each get to contribute to it in the way we enjoy—or at least don't mind—by getting the benefit of what the other one does, too.

That's how product teams and the design system team should work together. Design system teams are really good at standardizing things and abstracting them. Product teams are really good at inventing new things and being able to use them in their products to meet their deadlines and to create customer value. Invest in this by letting it drive your Measuring Spoon Cycle.

Once this cycle is going, design system contribution becomes automatic just by virtue of everyone doing the work they're supposed to do. From a product team's perspective, they created some things for a feature for their customers, and a few weeks later, it shows up in the design system, ready for other teams to use. From a design system team's perspective, all they had to do was identify some good component and pattern candidates and make a few tweaks to make sure the component's scope is a little more widely applicable. When done well, it feels like magic to everyone involved, but it's really because everyone's doing their part.

When Should These Design System Activities Be Done?

If the "who" part of design systems is the biggest thing most teams get wrong, the "when" part is the second largest culprit that goes hand-in-hand. In expecting product teams to abstract, contribute, and document components that could go into the system, that work is often expected to happen at the end of a product design cycle. Ha! As if product teams had extra time. And even if they did, they're probably sprinting to the finish line of their work and would much rather spend the extra time getting to the things they initially had to deprioritize because of the deadline, not doing an act of kindness for a team they're not on with results they won't see. The end of a project is one of the worst times to ask any team to do cleanup.

A few years ago, my team and I went to Orlando, Florida's Disney World to speak at and attend a design conference. We were also at the tail end of some product work we had been doing, and the only thing we hadn't finished was our documentation work. While everyone went to Disney World the next day, we sat in our hotel rooms, documenting APIs and UX guidelines. Every time I think of saving the documentation part for last, I remember that I'd rather go to Disney World instead. True story.

If abstraction and contribution and documentation don't go at the end of the process, when should they happen? All throughout.

I can hear you scoffing already. "Sure! Document throughout a project! Just like flossing every day and balancing your checkbook once a week." Fair enough, dear reader! In order to make this a habit, you'll have to formalize it a bit. If you're onboard with everything you've read in this chapter so far, you realize that design system work and product design work are all part of the same process. Contribution isn't a separate effort; it's a step in the piloting process.

Allot time for both "Flow weeks" and "Systems weeks" (Figure 6.5). Give the product teams 2–3 weeks to get into the flow of solving user needs. In those Flow weeks, the design system team can surface and provide existing components and patterns that save time for those product teams. Then, every 3–4 weeks, the design system team does a Systems week, a week where they get to audit any newly created components from any of the three pilot teams for eligibility in the design system.

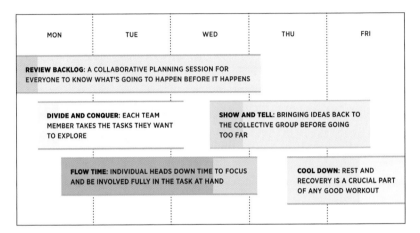

FIGURE 6.5A

Magic happens when a connected and safe team gets into a state of flow.

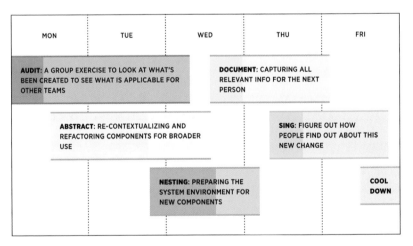

FIGURE 6.5B

Product work is most important because it's a direct line to creating customer value, but scaling good product work for future benefit needs allotted time. Plan a Systems week: One week out of every four to extract and abstract the great work being done so that others can make use of it, too.

The criteria for eligibility is simple. For each component candidate, ask, "Can three other teams at this company use this component right now?" If not, don't add it to the design system.

Bring on the groans. "What strict criteria! Surely, we have to be more forward thinking than that?" I get the sentiment. But a strict rule helps avoid the trap most organizations fall into. Remember, most design system graveyards are full of design systems that have lots of components that no one uses. The nuance is that they're full of components that someone might use someday. But "someday" never arrives. By keeping your design system contribution criteria focused on the needs *right now*, you're much more poised to create a system that gets immediately adopted because the need is immediate.

(That said, when I work with teams that understand that nuance, then we'll slightly expand the criteria to be, "Can another team at this company use this component this quarter?" Yeah, I'm a big softy.)

For all of the components that do fit the criteria of being used now or within the quarter, the rest of this Systems week gives the design system the time to take components that were likely made for a specific use case and abstract the design and code to be more broadly applicable and flexible for other teams. This is also the week to write any relevant documentation for just a handful of new components, as opposed to waiting until the end of a whole product cycle and needing to write documentation for dozens or even hundreds of new components. (Remember and say it with me: "We want to go to Disney World.")

Systems week doesn't just make time for the abstraction and documentation work; it carves out space to spread the word about the newly available updates. If a component falls in the forest…the analogy stinks but hopefully you get the idea. Tell people there are new options available to them! Every organization will have a different vehicle for this among email updates, Slack channel posts, wiki entries, show-and-tell ceremonies, and much more. But the important thing here is that there's dedicated time allocated to effort that often gets left until last.

And maybe you could floss your teeth a little more, too.

Where and How Should These Design System Activities Be Done?

Phew! That's a lot of paradigm shifting in the "who" and "when" of design systems.

Luckily, I can ease off the gas in this "where" and "how" section. While the "who" and "when" are the stuff teams usually get wrong, the "where" and "how" are the stuff that usually goes well! Your organization probably already has a decent starting point of a product design process that defines a lot of the "where" and "how" already:

- How should we review ongoing work as a team?
- Where do we build our prototypes?
- How can our executive sponsors track our work?
- Where do customers go to give feedback on new product features?

Hopefully, you have a confident reaction looking at this list, because these are the kinds of things that are already figured out at your organization. And they have a place in the workflow, too; these are the kinds of best practices that your design system team can "collect" as things to continue doing. These are the kinds of ways that product design influences the design system, and the design system influences product design. It's that healthy mix of some new things and some established things that give you good momentum for the next product cycle.

A Design System Governance and Contribution Template

That's a lot to digest! How do you put it all together?

Pick a date for your first Systems week. The first activity of this first Systems week will be to document—no, chronicle—how you currently work. Resist the urge to create a new way of working, even if your current process is less than ideal. If you can't resist that urge, document two versions: the current process and the new, ideal one. Document the what, why, who, when, where and how of each activity. As a starting point, you can use this extensive starting point/flowchart (Figure 6.6).

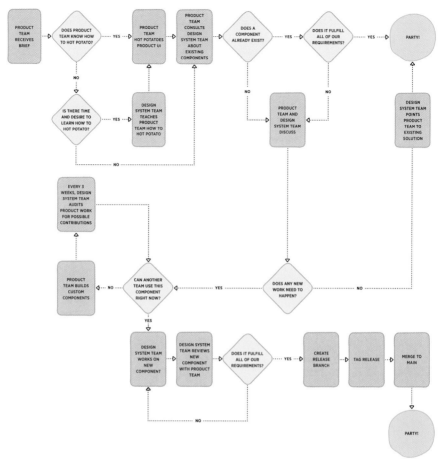

FIGURE 6.6
A flowchart for how design system teams and product teams can work together.

A lot of what's in this template will be irrelevant or inappropriate to your organization. That's OK; prioritize documenting what's more fitting for you over sticking to the items in this template. It matters less what you specifically do. It matters more that you all agree on something. Whatever you agree on, document it. Just like the piloting process, do a thing, and then write it down. After the first Systems week is over, try to follow the process you captured in the next Flow week. Make edits and additions in the next Systems week (or sooner) as you discover them. This is how you build the organization muscles and habits to move past a design system as a tool and more into how design systems can become an ingrained practice.

Design System as Canon and the Expanded Universe

The *Star Wars* saga by George Lucas has been a cultural tidal wave since the original movie debuted in 1977. Since then, a plethora of stories have been written about the *Star Wars* universe and characters, some by Lucasfilm (and later by acquiring company Disney) and others by other companies and the general fan population. Which begs the question: Which stories are "official," and which are not?

To answer that question, Lucasfilm established the idea of "canon" in 1994. As defined by online encyclopedia Wookiepedia, *Star Wars* canon is the set of immovable objects of *Star Wars* history, the characters and events to which all other tales must align. *Star Wars* canon includes the six *Star Wars* films; the *Star Wars: The Clone Wars* television series and film; novels (where they align with what is seen on-screen); and Part I of the short story *Blade Squadron*. In short, canon is gospel. Everything else is considered part of the "Expanded Universe" (later rebranded to "Legends"), i.e., they're allowed and encouraged to exist even though they're not part of canon.

The overall awareness of *Star Wars* generally reflects canon, too (Figure 6.7). Most people know canon characters Darth Vader and Princess Leia and Luke Skywalker and Yoda, but Expanded Universe characters Cindel Towani or DRN-38 or Nadia Grell are much less familiar, even though they're crucial to their storylines.

The model of what is and isn't canon holds well for design systems as well. At every point, your design system should contain what's canon, the official components and patterns and processes to which everything else must align.

That doesn't mean that everything has to go in the design system. In fact, some stuff shouldn't go into the design system. Every organization needs an expanded universe of components, ones that are crucial to their own local stories.

Deciding what components, patterns, and processes get promoted to canon through a pilot-based governance and contribution workflow is how your design system starts to become the story of how your organization makes valuable digital interfaces for your customers.

FIGURE 6.7

Canon and noncanon *Star Wars* characters are pictured here. Clockwise from top left: Nadia Grell, Darth Vader, BZ-9D, Yoda, Dash Rendar, Princess Leia.

Questions for Reflection

- Start filling out the governance and contribution template with your team. How standardized is this workflow across the organization? What can you do to move more teams closer to one official story of how you make digital interfaces?

- Among the "who," "what," "where," "when," and "why" of governance, which one has been or will be easiest for you and your team? Which one has been or will be the most difficult?

CHAPTER 7

Roles and Responsibilities

Seventeen software engineers met in early 2001 to discuss how work could and should get done, and out popped the "Manifesto for Agile Software Development"—often shortened to "The Agile Manifesto"—a series of principles and guidelines to shepherd software projects. The manifesto led with these four main tenets:

- Individuals and interactions over processes and tools
- Working software over comprehensive documentation
- Customer collaboration over contract negotiation
- Responding to change over following a plan

Many organizations have adopted Agile wholesale as their standard of shipping software, so design system practices need to effectively fit within the context of Agile. When it comes to design systems, my favorite Agile Manifesto principle and the one I focus on most is the second, because it's the one that most teams seem to forget and the one that unlocks the most benefits when done well. The manifesto makes a point to say, "While there is value in the items on the right, we value the items on the left more." But most design system teams and product teams seem to indicate that documentation is more important than working software.

Don't believe me? Look at the output that team members are responsible for. Information architects make diagrams. Writers make documents. Product managers write requirements. Strategists craft briefs. Designers make comps. Engineers write code.

Who on the team actually makes working software? Only the engineers. Every other role is largely one of documentation (Figure 7.1). What is a wireframe? Documentation about how a site or an app should function. What is a comp? Documentation about what a piece of software should look like.

Working software over comprehensive documentation? Doesn't look like it, according to our team makeup. Every role primarily makes documentation except engineers. Most teams are overindexed on documenters.

It often doesn't look like teams value software over documentation, according to the time spent on a project or sprint. Engineers often get the least amount of time on a project. Extra time spent on discovery or design usually eats into engineering time without moving a deadline or reducing scope. These are the kinds of signals that indicate where priority truly lies.

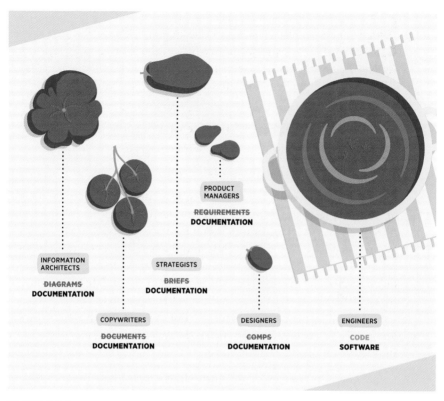

FIGURE 7.1

Most digital team members make documentation, but only engineers make code, the real thing for users to interact with.

Prioritizing working software is prioritizing things that your organization's customers can use. The more time your team spends writing documentation—especially documentation that's created before software is made—the longer it will take for customers to interact with your products. This is why the piloting we discussed in Chapter 5, "Pilots—The Best Way to Start and Sustain a Design System," is so important: it prioritizes adoption and use as quickly as possible. If your organization has a culture of documentation over software, you can model the opposite—a culture of relentless focus on shipping working software—by starting it with your design system team.

The irony of our industry's ever-expanding team roles is that there's only one role that you need on a team: the one that writes HTML.

Front-end Engineering Is More Important Than Visual Design

In 2005, developer Noah Stokes created a marvel of a personal website (Figure 7.2).

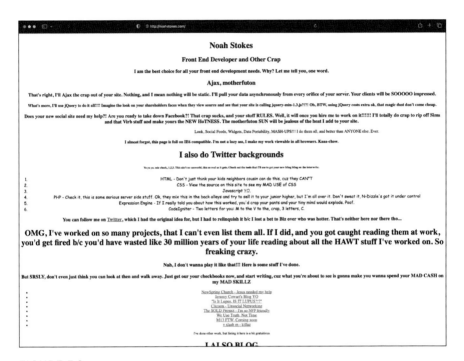

FIGURE 7.2
Noah Stokes's 2005 website is a full product.

Noah's website was just HTML. There's no CSS file attached to it. There's some animation of a line that goes back and forth from the left to the right edges of the screen, but it's not powered by fancy new CSS or JavaScript animation...it's a good ol' <marquee> element.

Noah's website is a complete product. Did he need a design comp? Nope. Could a designer have made this website better? Possibly. (Although there's a good argument for why this is probably the best this site could be.) Could an information architect make this better? Probably. Could more backend logic make this better? Probably. But all the things that I'm talking about are to make it better, not to make it. Design, IA, strategy: all of those are optimizations on software. And as every good engineer knows, you optimize afterward.

You don't start by optimizing; there's nothing to optimize yet. What does a true, minimal viable web product look like? A plain old HTML document.

When it comes to making web products, front-end engineering is more important than visual design.

"But Dan…can you really draw that conclusion from a personal website created in 2005?" Fair point, dear reader. Allow me to point you to some more supporting evidence.

The general public often forgets that entrepreneur and investor Jeff Bezos started as computer engineer Jeff Bezos. The first Amazon website launched in 1995 was just HTML with a handful of HTML-based styling attributes (Figure 7.3). Bezos's original job postings on Usenet for help with the product asked for "C/C++/Unix developers" who have "familiarity with web servers and HTML." No mention of design or strategy or anything like that; they weren't necessary to create the foundations for one of the most influential products in the history of the world.

FIGURE 7.3
The original Amazon.com from 1995.

(What's really gonna break your brain is the fact that many of the world's most popular software products—eBay, Craigslist, Wikipedia—still stay pretty faithful to their original "undesigned" forms. Could there be a tie between the ones who best understand the idea of prioritizing working software and those who have lasting success?)

Front-end Engineering Is More Important Than Back-end Engineering

Developer Mandy Michael wrote a fantastic article in 2017 entitled "Is There Any Value in People Who Cannot Write JavaScript?" where she lamented the fact that the majority of current job openings necessitate JavaScript knowledge.[1] I think part of the subtext that Mandy was raising is this: Are HTML and CSS as important as JavaScript?

I say, "Heck yes!"

Back-end languages—and I sort of include JavaScript in there for now—are incredibly powerful, but there's a reason that all of them have at least one method of outputting HTML. Until you output HTML—whether it's the Echo function in PHP or Return method in React, or whatever language you're using—the product isn't a real web product until you put something on the screen that people can interact with. And what is that thing? HTML. Whether generated by the server or the client, you need HTML to use anything on the web. When I'm talking to or working with people who are new to the industry and they ask me what's the first thing they should learn, I always say HTML. If you're trying to make web products, all roads lead to HTML.

When it comes to making web products, front-end languages are more important than back-end languages.

Front-end Engineering: The Missing Skill Set

If your team consists of designers that work in tools like Figma or Sketch and you also have engineers that configure Webpack builds and write .net or Java, you're missing a core skill set that will allow you to take the most advantage of a design system.

In order to make the most of a design system, you have to prioritize front-end development.

That might mean expanding your designers' responsibilities to include coding HTML and CSS, or convincing everyone that

---

1   Mandy Michael, "Is There Any Value in People Who Cannot Write JavaScript?" September 13, 2017, **https://medium.com/@mandy.michael/ is-there-any-value-in-people-who-cannot-write-javascript-d0a66b16de06**

front-end is "real programming," or hiring front-end engineers that already have that specialty. Either way, you have to invest in front-end design and development. It's the coupling that connects design, engineering, and customers (Figure 7.4). Without that investment, you're missing the most critical part of how digital products built with design systems can create customer value.

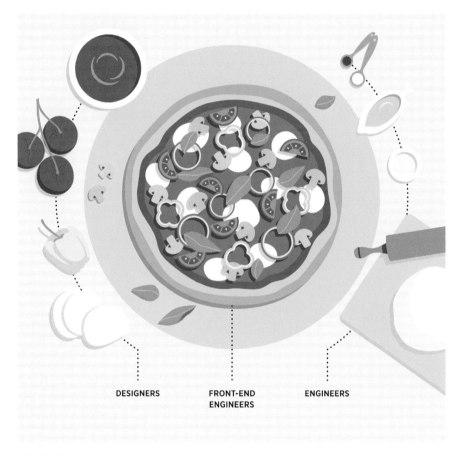

FIGURE 7.4
Front-end is where design and engineering converge.

Rebranding the "Front-end Engineer"

On May 11, 1996, ValuJet Flight 592 was supposed to fly from Miami to Atlanta. Instead, tragically, it crashed in the Florida Everglades, with no survivors among the 110 passengers and crew. Following the crash, despite initially ruling the airline safe, the FAA grounded

ValuJet flights for three months. Upon further investigation, the FAA found that ValuJet often utilized dangerous cost-cutting measures. They didn't train employees well and relied on the cheapest labor they could find for maintenance. The company quickly developed a reputation for its delinquent safety. When people thought of ValuJet, they thought of untrustworthiness. That was the gut feeling people had about it; untrustworthiness was its brand.

In 1997—a year later—ValuJet acquired AirTran Airways, and they actually took the smaller airline's name. The original name was too toxic to keep around. The brand of ValuJet had become synonymous with danger. They had to rebrand because they had to change people's gut feeling about them.

Unfortunately, there's another name that's starting to become toxic in our industry. It's well-intentioned and it actually does mean what it's supposed to, but despite the best of intentions, our industry is starting to have the wrong gut feeling about it.

I think it's time to rebrand the "front-end engineer."

The title is starting to have the connotation that front-end skills aren't useful skills. We're never more than a few days away from Twitter arguments about whether writing HTML and CSS is "real programming." Ugh. (It is.)

We want a title that says that the skills this person possesses are important. We might even acknowledge that it's not the same as other programming, but it's equally as valuable, if not more or even most valuable, as I made an argument for in the beginning of this chapter. We want to communicate that this person is involved in crafting the product vision, as well as the interface the users will interact with.

If you think about it for a bit, you'll realize that lots of organizations already have a word for this. That word is…

Designer.

When I'm working with teams that want to be more collaboratively successful at making web products, one of the first things I suggest is moving all front-end engineers to the design team and changing their titles to "Designer." It takes a little while to warm up to the idea and a little more time to implement, but it's amazing to see how much confidence a front-end engineer can get when people think of them—and when they think of themselves—as designers.

It's easy to justify, too.

Front-end Engineers as Designers

Look across your current design team. Perhaps one of your designers, Kate, uses Sketch. Maybe another designer, Miles, uses Photoshop (I know, I know). Yet another designer, Kamala, uses Figma.

It's easy to make a case for why front-end engineer Jane—who primarily uses HTML5 as her design tool—can join this team as a designer, too. All of these people design interfaces for users. All of them use different tools. But because they're all different, they're all the same: they're all designers (Figure 7.5).

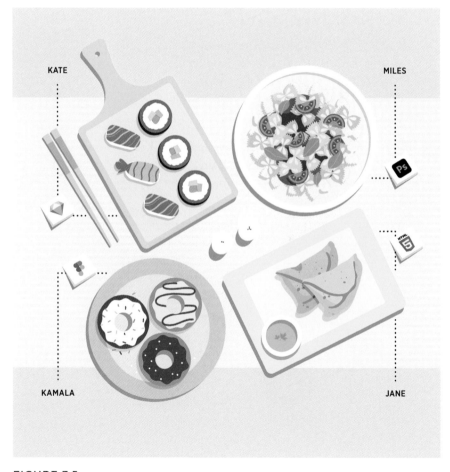

FIGURE 7.5
Diverse teams allow people to be different in a way that's delicious together.

What's that you say? Everyone on your design team uses Sketch because it's more efficient when everyone's alike? You're right: that would make it difficult for Jane to join this team, because she's different from everyone else. And that's how easy it is to eliminate diversity from a team. When you force—or worse, encourage—people who think and act the same to group together, it very obviously leaves out the ones who aren't like everyone else (Figure 7.6). It creates outcasts. It creates stale and mundane thinking.

But if you can shape a group with different skills and different backgrounds and different approaches, now you've got something really special. This is a really effective way to design a team.

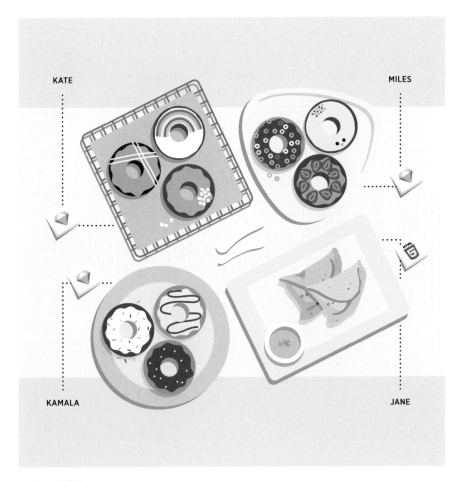

FIGURE 7.6
Making people assimilate to be the same easily creates outcasts.

Compare this to the way we typically design our teams. We try to make the categories really specific but the skills really broad within them. Like, if you're a visual designer, you have to be all of a visual designer.

This rarely works because people don't fit neatly into little boxes. Scott Belsky, the founder of work showcase site Behance and chief product officer at Adobe, describes it like this: "...a lot of the magic I've observed in teams over the years happens when the talent stack is collapsed—when a designer also codes, when an engineer has a growth hack skill set, when a product leader is great at copy. unfortunately (sic), traditional org structures are liable to suppress such overlaps of roles instead of running w/ them. but the best modern orgs tailor the structure of each product team to the actual people and overlaps they're lucky enough to have."

Inevitably, you'll have a visual designer who can do a little UX, too, but can't art direct very well yet. Or a front-end engineer who doesn't know JavaScript but is really into deployment tools (Figure 7.7).

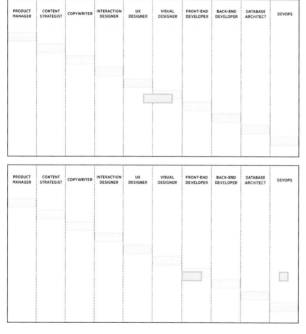

FIGURE 7.7
Making people fit neatly into boxes means everyone falls short.

Rather than making the boxes specific and trying to fill them broadly, do the opposite: make the roles broad and then fill them specifically.

One configuration I've recommended is that every maker on the team is either a designer or an engineer. Think of this more like a spectrum than binary. Plot people, not roles. Think of it like a heat map (Figure 7.8).

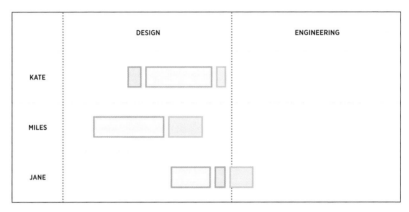

FIGURE 7.8
When the roles are broad, people can occupy their own space within them.

- Kate is a strong user interface designer and can do a lot of UX thinking on her own. She can even tweak some CSS to get the details right if someone else can initially write it.
- Miles is kind of an old-school art director: he likes writing his own copy while doing broad stroke design, but he's the first to admit that he's not good at the details.
- Jane does most of her designing in the browser and CodePen with HTML and CSS. She knows a tiny bit about writing JavaScript from scratch but is pretty proficient editing it and finding snippets on the web to drop in and modify.

Jane blurs the lines between design and engineering, but because her skills fall more on the design end than engineer, she can call herself a designer. It's her choice.

This is a much more realistic visualization of your team's strengths and weaknesses.

This is also only one version of a spectrum. Instead of plotting against a "design to engineering" spectrum, you can map this to your delivery process (Figure 7.9)—for example: planning, sketching, building, deploying. And you'll see that this is much more of a continuum than specific sections. Planning blends right into sketching, which blends into building.

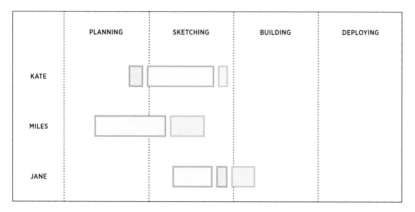

FIGURE 7.9
There are many more configurations for where people fit on a team other than just job descriptions.

Perhaps converting front-end engineers to designers is more than your organization can culturally stomach right now. That's fair! Here are some alternate ways to make a framing shift for the role of front-end engineer that may be easier to implement.

Front of the Front-End

Front-end designer Brad Frost quipped on web development podcast "ShopTalk Show" that "front-end engineering" should be split into "front-of-the-front-end" and "back-of-the-front-end,"[2] and those terms seemed to have gained traction! He then went on to define those terms, both collectively and individually:

- A front-of-the-front-end developer determines the look and feel of a button, while a back-of-the-front-end developer determines what happens when that button is clicked.

---

2   "334: How to Think like a Front-End Developer with Brad Frost," *ShopTalk Show*, October 22, 2018, **https://shoptalkshow.com/334/**

- A front-of-the-front-end developer is a web developer who specializes in writing HTML, CSS, and presentational JavaScript code.
- A back-of-the-front-end developer is a web developer who specializes in writing JavaScript code necessary to make a web application function properly.

Consider adding these terms to your team's vocabulary—if not official titles—to create clarity in roles and responsibilities.

The Hammer and the Chisel

Sparkbox is an agency in Dayton, Ohio, that does excellent web and design system work. They have these concepts called the "Hammer and the Chisel."[3] These aren't titles, mind you: they still have titles like "Frontend Designer" and "Developer," but "Hammer" and "Chisel" describe how they think of their work.

Here's how front-end designers Philip Zastrow and Andrew Spencer describe it: "The Hammer puts in the overall HTML and CSS structure for our base of layout and overall look and feel of components. The Chisel takes the Hammer's work and refines it and makes it more polished and aligned with the original design vision. It puts a client in a better position to see the progress of the site and see refinement throughout the process. They can see the vision come to life."

Psychological Safety

In 2013, a team within Google's People Operations—that's Google's version of "human resources"—set out to determine what makes for effective teams at Google. Their hypothesis was that it would be something like a good mix of seniority, skill, enthusiasm, and motivation.

But that wasn't the case at all. What turned out to be the most successful predictor of top performing teams? Psychological safety. Teams where people felt safe—where they wouldn't get fired or ridiculed or ostracized for their ideas, work, and selves—were the highest performing.

Changing your workflow and team dynamic isn't just to make design and development better and faster. Work should be more exciting,

---

3   Philip Zastrow, "The Hammer and the Chisel," May 30, 2017, https://sparkbox
.com/foundry/the_hammer_and_the_chisel

fulfilling, innovative, and ultimately fun. That starts with safety, knowing that you're all in it together, and you have each other's backs.

In order to start creating more safety within your teams, be the first to extend that safety to others. Many teams employ the Agile ritual of "daily standups," using a format of sharing what you did yesterday, what you're doing today, and what blockers stand in your way. Add this new part: What risk did I take yesterday? This will both normalize that taking risks is a part of everyone's job as well as allow everyone an equal opportunity to share their successes and failures. Not every risk is worth taking, and not every risk turns out to be a success. That's OK. Expose the dynamic that it's OK.

While I've rarely met anyone that disagrees with the general idea of supporting more psychological safety within their teams, the specific places that the obstacles sneak up in design system work are worth addressing. One of the first places to look is where a new skill is being attempted. To our workflow changes, this might be the first time a designer has written a line of code. If you're an engineer, your first instinct might be to critique that code to point out how it could be better. Beware though: even though your intention may be pure, a criticism this early on may discourage that designer more than encourage them and signal that they shouldn't have tried something new here. Instead of criticizing the code, praise the person. Build up their confidence in trying something new so that they're more prone to do it again and again.

The same could be true of an engineer who has made a design decision, something they may not be used to doing. Instead of saying that it still looks bad—which it likely will on a first try—affirm the attempt. These affirmations set a foundation of safety for your colleagues that will make your collaborations on working software that much more productive.

If you're a manager, lead by example. If you're not a manager, lead by example. Just start doing it. You'll see everyone start to join in after a few weeks.

Ecosystem Engineers

Beavers are fascinating, aren't they? They build dams, mostly for protection and also to make sure they have food when it gets colder.

Even though it's not their intention, many other species benefit from what they build. Woodpeckers occupy the trees that beavers excavate. Ducks and geese settle in their old lodges. Their wetlands become homes for herons, kingfishers, frogs, lizards, dragonflies, mussels, beetles, and more.

Dr. Clive Jones at the Cary Institute of Ecosystem Studies came up with a name for beaver-like creatures who create habitats for others to flourish. He calls them "ecosystem engineers."

Isn't that a great name for the people who either intentionally or unintentionally create the habitat for others to flourish? I know many a designer that would and have traded invention for habitat-building. During one of my interviews at Facebook years ago, I remember asking a very talented designer what was interesting to them about working there. They replied, "Having the ability to roll out a feature to 100 million users? There's no bigger rush."

Ecosystem engineers are interested in building platforms…quite literally, "a raised level surface on which people or things can stand." Thirty years ago, Sir Tim Berners-Lee used the existing technology of HTTP and a newly transformed version of SGML called HTML and stacked them together as a platform to create the World Wide Web. Fifteen years ago, it only took six months to build the initial version of YouTube because it stood on the existing platform of the web.

If you're the kind of person who likes building platforms to help others succeed, a design system team might be the right place for you.

Three-legged Stools

In his article "Defining Product Design," former VP of Design at Airbnb Alex Schleifer describes the making of a good product like this:[4]

> Three elements define a product: the business, the code, and the pixels. Give each a voice in all product decisions. Fuse Engineering, Product, and Design from the start.

> The team should resemble a three-legged stool, in which each leg represents one of the three areas that helps build a product. If it's done from the start, each function can grow in parallel and proper ratio as the broader organization scales.

---

4 Alex Schleifer, "Defining Product Design: A Dispatch from Airbnb's Design Chief," **https://review.firstround.com/defining-product-design-a-dispatch-from-airbnbs-design-chief**

Without those strategies from the onset, you're bound to create an unstable stool down the line, which, in this case, is a shaky product. That might be because no design role was developed at the onset or was added on after the product—and the engineering and product management teams—has already matured and grown. The best way to avoid a wobbly seat (or product) is to build each stool with three legs from the get-go.

Design systems intentionally blend Design, Engineering, and Product in order to succeed. Great design system teams balance growing the team with an eye toward how Design, Engineering, and Product are doing at the organization so the design system team can be in lockstep with them...not behind, but not ahead either.

Creating or even using a design system one phase at a time is like building a stool one leg at a time; the only time the stool is stable is at the very end. Instead, following a more collaborative workflow always keeps the stool balanced and growing at a steady, equivalent rate.

Other Roles on a Design System Team

Earlier in the chapter, I highlighted the importance of a close-knit designer + engineer workflow. It's no surprise then that design system teams often start with these two roles. Where does the team go from there? How and when does a design system team grow beyond this?

The Product Owner

Generally, the next role to add is a design system product owner. Design and engineering are often very tactical roles, and so they tend to want or need a product owner or someone who can walk the hallways and do some of the evangelism while they're actually doing some of the "on-the-ground" work of componentry (Figure 7.10).

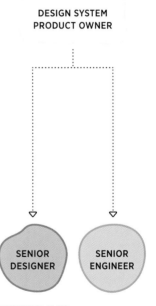

FIGURE 7.10
A product owner is usually the first role needed on a design system team outside of a founding designer and engineer.

That product owner can come from many different places for many different reasons:

- The original designer or engineer on this team may become the product owner. This kind of design system product owner tends to excel at fielding requests from features teams, largely because of their history, context, and familiarity with the system.

- An external product manager may join the team to become the product owner, turning the original dynamic duo into a trio, commonly known as the famed *product triad* structure. This kind of product owner fits well on a team where the original designer and engineer have little familiarity or interest in focusing on business outcomes.

- An external product manager with design, engineering, or product background may join the team in more of a management capacity. This kind of product owner works well with team members who may be talented but need some structure and support to continue to get things done.

The most important job of a product owner on a design system team is to understand how to weave the design system into the way business gets done at the organization. That means understanding feature teams' roadmaps, as well as the design system team members' capabilities, enough to plot out where the two can naturally intersect.

More Engineering and Design Help

For successful design system teams that start to see more interest from feature teams, the workload tends to grow. Generally, that starts on the engineering side: give us more components we can implement into our features. Another engineer helps alleviate that burden to share the work with the initial engineer (Figure 7.11). Design help often goes hand-in-hand with that.

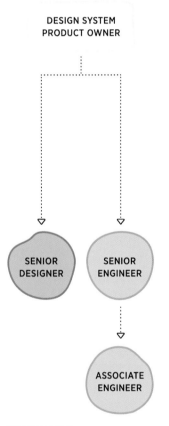

FIGURE 7.11
More production help is often needed as a design system grows.

Producers/Project Managers

The next stage tends to see a need for some more on-the-ground management. This is different from the design system product owner, whose focus is on talking to other teams and evangelizing it as a whole, but teams often need someone to help manage the work at an in-the-weeds level as the team grows. That role is often a producer or project manager (Figure 7.12) who ties all of the individual threads together to make sure that it's all moving toward the product owner's vision for the design system. For teams that are run in an Agile way, the producer/project manager is often a scrum master, someone who facilitates activities and rituals like sprint planning and standup for the team.

This person may also be a DesignOps professional. In the words of Atlassian's Head of DesignOps, Dominique Ward, DesignOps is the organization typically charged with "designing design and designing designers." DesignOps governs areas like design process, team structure and culture, hiring, and design tools—which may include design systems, among other things. (See sidebar: "A Conversation with Michelle Chin about DesignOps.")

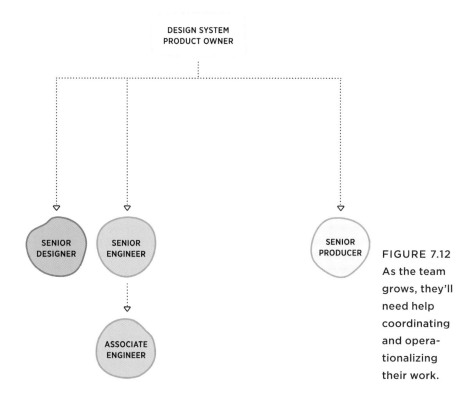

FIGURE 7.12 As the team grows, they'll need help coordinating and operationalizing their work.

Michelle Chin is a design advocate at zeroheight, a design system documentation platform. She's been a product designer, design manager, DesignOps manager, strategist, and more. I asked her a few questions about her experience with DesignOps and why it's so important.

What is DesignOps?

DesignOps is the specialized support services that help ensure that the design team can do its best. If you consider individual contributors on the design team (e.g., designers, researchers, content people, etc.) as professional athletes, DesignOps people are the athletic trainers, nutritionists, etc. They have special skills that allow individual contributors to focus on their craft and set them up for success.

What has your experience with DesignOps been like?

There's DesignOps as a role, and there's DesignOps the work. So even when I wasn't in a specific DesignOps role, I usually did some operational work to help improve team processes. While working at Citrix, some DesignOps side projects included creating checklists to ensure accessibility design, new hire onboarding, or facilitating workshops to help define our team's critique culture.

When I became a design manager at Citrix, DesignOps became a more official part of my work. However, as design managers, so much of our work focused on design strategy and people management that we often neglected DesignOps projects. We tried to fit in initiatives where we could but never felt we could give them the proper attention. As a manager, you want to do right by your team, and knowing you weren't didn't feel great.

I attended the DesignOps Summit a few times and always wondered if DesignOps was something I could pursue. I loved managing and guiding people in their careers, but I saw DesignOps as a way to help empower individual contributors (ICs) even further. I worked with my manager on evolving my career toward a DesignOps path.

We figured out how to make DesignOps a practice on our team. Our idea proposed that the DesignOps responsibility usually asked of design managers would shift solely to me. It would give them more time to focus on design strategy and people management. Then I could exclusively concentrate on DesignOps, and we could get several design org initiatives done with the attention and quality the team deserved.

I absolutely loved this transition and had so much fun in my role. In some ways, it felt like finding my "true calling." Unlike my work designing enterprise software, I saw my "users" (the design team) daily. So, I could see the direct impact I was making and had first-hand visibility for when we needed to pivot. Knowing I was helping them succeed at doing amazing design work felt satisfying.

There were certainly challenges, though. I was a DesignOps team of one, and DesignOps was a new concept for many. So, in addition to driving initiatives and working on projects, I did a lot of educating, advocating, and expectation-setting not just within the design org but also with other departments. It was also tough being a team of one. Because I was the only one leading an org-wide initiative, people often thought it was a personal project. So, some felt it was less of a priority when the project was really to benefit the whole team. I still enjoyed it, and even as a team of one, I found friends through the DesignOps Assembly Slack community.

I ended up pivoting away from DesignOps when I joined zeroheight. My focus is more on consulting, writing best practices, and building a community. But my role as a design advocate leans heavily into my experience in DesignOps and design systems. But it's hard to give up once you develop a knack for operationalizing. I'm constantly trying to find ways to improve processes for our team.

How do DesignOps and Design Systems relate to one another?

In some ways, DesignOps relates to design systems; in others, they don't. Philosophically, people can see design systems as a solution that helps ICs/teams work more effectively to focus on solving challenges. In that respect, it's like DesignOps.

But fundamentally, a considerable amount of design work is involved in creating a design system. Unless the DesignOps person was previously a designer, it would be challenging for them to contribute to building the actual parts of the design system. Design systems can happen without having a design, code, or content background.

That's not to say design systems don't need DesignOps. It's the opposite. DesignOps people can contribute to design systems in many other ways. They're essential in scaling a design system and design system team. For example, their expertise can help identify and create governance processes, manage the team's workload and backlog, coordinate with cross-functional partners, and increase adoption.

continues

How is DesignOps different from Design or Product Design?

DesignOps is more like service design; both are design and product design adjacent. So, you often apply the same design thinking principles: understand your users, brainstorm solutions, pilot ideas, etc. Instead of creating solutions as a feature or app, your solutions are templates, processes, or playbooks. Many DesignOps practitioners were previously designers. So, I think of it as being a designer with different tools and challenges.

What areas are DesignOps concerned with?

This can feel muddy when there's a small team, and DesignOps people feel like they do a little of everything. But there are two focus areas of DesignOps: TeamOps and ProductOps.

In TeamOps, practitioners focus on holistic initiatives that benefit the design org horizontally. Some aspects include hiring, onboarding, tool procurement, team culture, learning and development, process standardization, design systems, budget, or illustration alignment. Anything that needs org-wide alignment is where they can help.

In ProductOps, practitioners work closely with designers supporting a specific product. So, they're more concerned with ensuring that designers can focus on getting their work done, removing blockers, and negotiating with cross-functional stakeholders. Depending on the company, they might handle project management tasks.

What traits, skills, or experience make for a successful DesignOps professional?

As you can imagine, DesignOps is a very people-oriented role. You can still be an introvert (like me) and do well, but the crucial skill you need is change management facilitation. Success is more than creating a process; it's getting people brought in and adjusted to the process.

In terms of traits, people who thrive in chaos do well. DesignOps people love jumping into a situation and figuring out how they can help create calm. Being flexible and easygoing helps, too. Implementing change is a process, and how teams react to change can differ from project to project. DesignOps people need to be flexible, patient, and ready to pivot.

When it comes to experience, having a design background is helpful in understanding context, having empathy, or building trust. But it's definitely not necessary! I've met some fantastic DesignOps people who came from nondesign disciplines.

Why is DesignOps important?

Overall, DesignOps helps keep a design team running smoothly. Although there might be no formal DesignOps role, someone is doing DesignOps work to help the team succeed. Even if the managers and ICs are more than capable of procuring software and other operational tasks, these tasks take up time, cause a lot of context switching, and distract them from their main responsibilities. Having DesignOps practitioners unburdens managers and ICs, so they can focus on their craft.

DesignOps as a role or team is also vital to help a team grow or maintain consistency at scale. When a dedicated team handles DesignOps, the org can stay aligned and adapt to changes (e.g., switching to a new tool) efficiently and smoothly.

What's easy about DesignOps?

The easiest thing about DesignOps is having access to your "users." As a product designer, we'd have to recruit users for any feedback, which takes time and effort. But in DesignOps, if I have a question, need feedback, or want to try something out, I only have to ping someone on Slack or drop in on a team meeting. I can also see how things work in real time to identify what's going well and where we may need to pivot.

What's difficult about DesignOps?

The hardest part is change management. Change can be difficult for people, even if they know it's for the better. For any arduous change, I try to make things fun and find time to celebrate any wins along the way. At a previous company, we were transitioning from several different cloud-based tools. People were skeptical the first time we migrated from one tool to its replacement. I get it, it was a lot of work, people would have to learn a whole new tool, and even though this is something they wanted, it never seems like a good time to shift workflows and mindsets. But to make things more enjoyable, we had working sessions, created Miro boards for adding GIFs and cocktail recipes based on their moods, and achievement boards for learning new skills. We even had a celebration party at the end and gave away prizes.

For the next tool transition, things were much more manageable. By then, DesignOps had built trust, and people knew we were trying to make things as painless as possible.

continues

What advice would you give to a team or organization that doesn't have a DesignOps team?

The size of a design org will indicate if they need a DesignOps person or team. If your team is rapidly growing, I'd strongly consider looking to add DesignOps. A good ratio might be one DesignOps person for every 1–2 design managers as a start. Because not everyone knows what DesignOps is or the value they bring, it can take a while to get the buy-in needed. Planting that seed earlier is helpful, so when the time for headcount comes up, the ask is not a surprise to anyone.

I'd also check in with your management team to see how they're doing. If they cannot get to the DesignOps projects they'd like to, it's a good sign that it's time to bring someone in. If you have someone internally interested in shifting to this role, it might be hard to make a case for this. It's not that the stakeholders disagree about the need for DesignOps. But they're more concerned about the gap this person would leave behind in their current role. So be prepared to have a plan for that.

What advice would you give to a team or organization that has DesignOps but isn't sure how to grow it?

If you have a large, mature DesignOps team, there are a lot of opportunities to grow the team. When UX was a budding field, most of us were generalists. But as more teams recognized user experience design, people could specialize in a specific aspect like information architecture, interaction design, or user research. Similarly, DesignOps people can start to specialize in ProductOps or TeamOps. I've even met people focusing on one specific aspect of TeamOps, like just tool procurement, just learning and development, or just event planning.

Once a DesignOps team matures, where there isn't constant chaos that needs wrangling, I think there are also more opportunities for DesignOps to become more strategic partners in growing the design org and educating and partnering with other cross-functional departments. Because of their experience with change management, they can help contribute ideas and weigh in on strategies that involve orchestrating change at scale.

Design and Engineering Hierarchy

With design system demand increasing and processes being put in place, production help becomes the largest need for the team. A few more designers and engineers help spread the workload around more evenly (Figure 7.13). This is also usually the point where you'll see a wider diversity of design and engineering challenges. Bringing more junior and mid-level designers and engineers onto the design system team to tackle the straightforward component work frees up the more senior designers and engineers to focus on more complex design and engineering challenges.

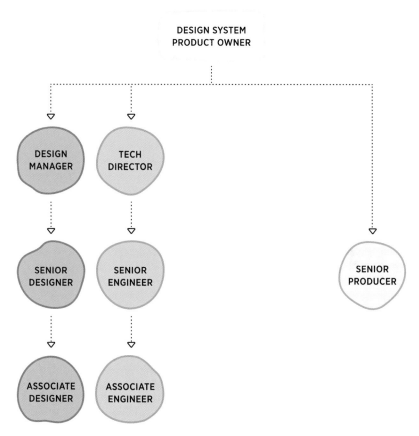

FIGURE 7.13

As the need for components increase, you'll need more production people to help keep up with the demand, as well as a hierarchy to support it.

More Than Just Design, Engineering, and Product

At this point, the workflow between the design system team and feature teams is usually pretty set or at least has a good rhythm being established. Component design and building, implementation, application, adoption…all of that stuff starts to get smoothed out. The design system team stops feeling like they're behind the needs of feature teams and for the first time feels like they're getting ahead and can take some deep breaths. This is the time you'll start to see some extracurricular activities come into play: office hours, design system newsletters and Slack channels, public design system roadmaps, etc.

It becomes more evident that other roles outside of the primary function of component design and building are critical: business analysis, content writing, quality assurance, etc. (Figure 7.14).

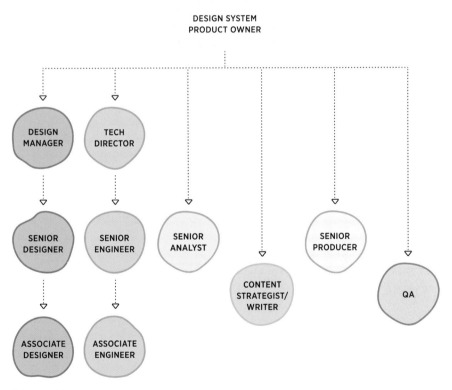

FIGURE 7.14
An org chart shows a fully cross-disciplinary design system team.

This is a version of what a mature design system team looks like: a full-service, holistic team that supports an organization-wide internal product. Most organizations I've worked with take between a year or two to grow to this point. While that might feel slow to some, it's important that this team grows organically with the need. Growing too fast or too slow puts this team out of sync with the rest of the organization, and that's the kiss of death for design system teams. The more connected a design system team is to the rest of the organization, the more successful and serving it can be.

Design System Annual Budgeting

Any digital product you use has a team of at least a few people that keep it bug-free and ideally even add useful features and functionality over time. In order for that to happen, the organization that supports digital product has to devote funds to it to keep it going. Design systems are products, and they're not exempt from this requirement.

Many teams starting a design system journey wonder what kind of funding they need to eventually allocate to sustain a design system practice. For those looking for a simple answer, it takes $1–$1.5 million annually to sustain a mature design system practice (Figure 7.15).

TEAM	
PRODUCT OWNER	$150K - $175K
DESIGN MANAGER	$120K - $150K
TECH DIRECTOR	$120K - $150K
SENIOR DESIGNER	$100K - $120K
SENIOR ENGINEER	$100K - $120K
SENIOR ANALYST	$100K - $120K
SENIOR PRODUCER	$100K - $120K
CONTENT STRATEGIST	$75K - $100K
ASSOCIATE DESIGNER	$70K - $90K
ASSOCIATE ENGINEER	$70K - $90K
QA	$70K - $90K
SOFTWARE AND LICENSES	$70K - $90K
TRAINING AND PROFESSIONAL DEVELOPMENT	$30K - $50K
TOTAL	**$1M - $1.5M** (ANNUALLY)

FIGURE 7.15

A sample annual budget for a mature, cross-disciplinary design system team.

Let's explore the nuances of that.

The salaries of the people on the team are the biggest cost of a design system. Because salaries vary widely between geographies and experience, there's a wide spread here for general applicability, but the good news is that your organization probably—hopefully?—has defined salary bands and levels, so you can plug in those ranges for a number that's realistic for your company.

The next largest cost will be training and professional development for the team. This team will be serving your entire organization at scale, so it's a worthwhile investment to keep them sharp and growing. That includes things like sending them to conferences, acquiring coaching, and having hundreds of copies of this book on hand (wink, wink).

The last big piece of budgeting for this team is software licenses. Just like a design system is an investment in a tool that makes other teams' jobs easier, this team will need their own tools. That includes software licenses, plug-ins, and other enterprise software for things like design software or project management tracking tools.

These dollar amounts aren't chump change. As described in the previous chapter, this is a big reason that trying to get buy-in for a design system effort before you've actually made any traction often flops: it's difficult to ask for $1 million without much to show. But if you can conduct some initial pilots and even measure the time savings, you can extrapolate that data and get a relatively realistic projection of the benefits of a design system at your organization. (In the next chapter, I'll give you a plethora of examples of things to track that make this case even stronger.)

One of my recent clients conducted a few pilots and used the tracked data to project a $40 million savings from an initial investment of $4 million. Assuming my math is right, that's a 1,000% return on investment. If that's not enough to whet your appetite, might I recommend you drop this book and pick up one about day trading instead?

Questions for Reflection

- Does your organization undervalue front-end engineering? How can you start to change the perception of value of front-end engineering?

- What roles currently exist on your design system team? Sketch out a timeline for when new people could join the team and the budget that needs to be allocated toward the growth of this team.

Process and Workflow for Design Systems

A ds from the 1920s were pretty simple. The tried-and-true formula was to describe a product's features as a way to appeal to the potential buyer. For example, an ad for the Randolph Radio Corporation's all-electric radio described its "no batteries, chargers, eliminators, acids, or liquids" as a headline (Figure 8.1). The rest of the ad highlighted the "beautiful ampliphonic console," "genuine walnut cabinets," and "7-tube radio." It was no frills... and no feelings.

In those days, a copywriter's job was to take what their clients wanted to say—usually simply the features of their product—and turn it into a headline and body copy. Then they'd hand that copy to an account executive who would run it to another floor and literally slide that paper under a door to the art department to "visualize" the final ad. Artists simply followed the copywriter's orders. It was very rare that the copywriter and the artist would actually know each other.

FIGURE 8.1
An ad for the Randolph
Radio Corporation
from the 1920s.

The accepted truth of advertising at the time was that copy was the idea and art was just the visuals that supported the idea. All of that changed when copywriter Bill Bernbach met art director Paul Rand. In their work, they sometimes thought the visuals could be the idea, or that the copy was the visuals. Rand once remarked about working with Bernbach, "This was my first encounter with a copywriter who understood visual ideas and who didn't come in with a yellow copy pad and a preconceived notion of what the layout should look like." Contrary to the siloed dynamic at the time, they'd take lunch breaks together to visit art museums and galleries; they became good friends.

That camaraderie led to a fresh new kind of advertising approach. Take, for example, an ad they created for Lee Hats (Figure 8.2). Rather than touting the features of the hat, the ad celebrated the company for hiring more workers and creating new jobs as a way to fight inflation. As far as visuals went, rather than showing an obvious picture of a hat, it displayed a solitary balloon, a symbol of the ad's concept that would resonate with its reader.

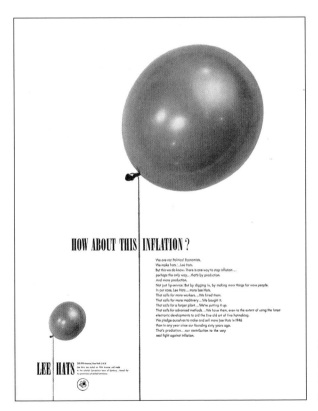

FIGURE 8.2
A new kind of ad for Lee Hats by Bernbach and Rand.

That kind of thinking changed the face of advertising forever. You may not have seen Lee Hats' ads before, but you likely have come across the famous "Lemon" ads for Volkswagen (Figure 8.3), created years later at the same agency DDB by Bernbach and Rand's professional descendants and protégés: copywriter Julian Koenig and art director Helmut Krone.

FIGURE 8.3
Famous Volkswagen ad from the 1960s.

Bernbach and Rand's collaborative working style led to the birth of the idea of "the creative team," the mutual respect and partnership between art director and copywriter that tended to yield unique results. Bob Gage, an art director who worked for DDB, the agency Bernbach co-founded, described it like this:

> Two people who respect each other sit in the same room for a length of time and arrive at a state of...free association, where the mention of one idea will lead to another idea, then to another. The art director might suggest a headline, the writer a visual. The entire ad is conceived as a whole, in a kind of ping-pong between disciplines.

Isn't that what we all strive for in our jobs? True collaboration with equals and partners? Ideas that build upon others? Why does this seem so far away for some of us? Unfortunately, the way the digital industry has evolved over the last few decades has led us to believe that increased separation in our disciplines is the path to success, when that actually couldn't be farther from the truth. One of the reasons I'm so excited about design systems is that they're an equally powerful and useful tool for both designers and engineers.

Design systems need multiple disciplines to work together closely to accomplish organization- and industry-changing work. Design systems need people like us to think differently about our craft than many currently think. We need to change the dynamic of how we work and move closer together as collaborative partners. If we can shift our thinking to embrace a different view of the roles of designers and engineers, a design system team can be a prototype of and breeding ground for the most Agile team within an organization.

Let's start by assessing the existing workflow between designers and engineers and look for opportunities to work more closely together.

Frameworks over Processes

Processes—a series of steps we can repeat to achieve a certain goal—give us comfort. It's no surprise that we look for processes wherever we can. Sadly, there is no one true process for making a design system. There's some amount of luck involved: getting lucky with team members' availability and capacity, roadmap timing with pilot teams, having the right executives involved to bless the ongoing efforts, and more. That's what makes design system work emergent, and that's what makes a process elusive.

However, where processes don't do well, as luck is involved, frameworks are a handy tool instead. A framework gives us a supporting structure that luck can flow through.

As an example, Newton's cradle (Figure 8.4) is a device where a sphere on one end is released and strikes other spheres that push the opposite end upward. As the last sphere returns, the cycle begins again. This is a process, a repeatable system that's optimized for efficiency, not innovation. It acts the same way every time. Nothing surprising ever occurs here.

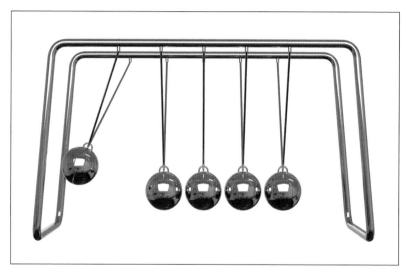

FIGURE 8.4
Newton's cradle is a predictable process.

However, a soccer field or football pitch (Figure 8.5) is a framework. Every game is played on the same kind of field of the same length. The rules are always the same. But what happens within the 90-minutes of the game is always emergent. It can't be fully predicted. We know what the outcomes will be—usually one winner and one loser—but how the game arrives there is what makes us all intrigued and enamored.

Despite logical reasons to the contrary, digital work still largely relies on a process, so we must deconstruct that process in order to move toward a framework that captivates us all. A simple Google image search for "digital design process" shows the kinds of steps that teams and organizations claim to follow to success (Figure 8.6).

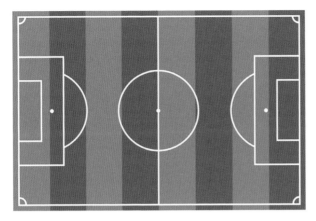

FIGURE 8.5
A football pitch/
soccer field is a set of
constraints that create
innovation.

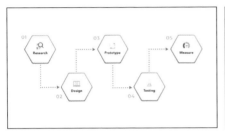

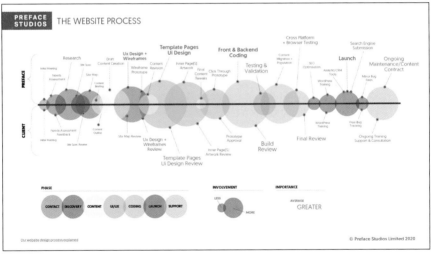

FIGURE 8.6
Typical results for "design process."

Where does this kind of "common wisdom" come from? Two places.

First, it comes from agencies. Take it from me, someone who ran an agency for a decade and has worked with and at other agencies for the decade before that. Agencies are incentivized to make their process look official and complicated so that clients think they can't do it on their own and also so they get paid a lot of money for it. I've been told by well-meaning clients—and also fought the urge regularly myself—to make the process graphic look prettier and more official so we could justify a higher price for our services.

The second place this comes from is less sleazy. In the 1970s, TRW Center Director of Engineering Dr. Winston Royce described his ideal process for working on space-flight systems. He was working on space-flight systems, and his job—as he stated in his paper—was to try to deliver projects "at an operational state, on-time, and within costs."[1] His paper described a flow that eventually came to be known as a "waterfall" process (Figure 8.7). He concluded his paper by saying, "I believe in this concept, but the implementation described is risky and invites failure." What a buzzkill!

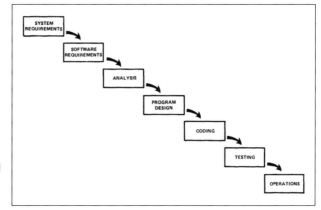

FIGURE 8.7
The original waterfall process from Dr. Winston Royce.

With initiatives as complex and emergent as design system work, it's difficult to rely on a process that will work every time. What's a better framework that we can use?

---

1   W. W. Royce, "Managing the Development of Large Software Systems," Proceedings of IEEE WESCON 26 (1970): 328–388.

My favorite answer comes from software engineer Jonathan Rasmusson in his book, *The Agile Samurai*. The first sentence of the first chapter of the book says, "What would it take to deliver something of value [to customers] each and every week?"

That's it. That's the framework. Every time your team sits down to work, ask this question. Whatever the answer, do that.

Less Is More

In order to do more working on software together, everyone has to do less of the old thing. Engineers need to spend less time waiting for "the design phase" to end to start building. Designers need to create fewer static comps. Restricting these wasteful activities frees up more time to do many more valuable things.

What kinds of valuable things? I'm so glad you asked.

The Hot Potato Process

I'd like to propose a new—and old—way for designers and engineers to be working together.

Pretend that you're making a web application for cataloging events and trips. You've done the research and have hypotheses to test through a minimum viable product (an MVP). What should you do next to bring this product to life?

For those of you who thought Figma or Sketch or Photoshop or some design tool, think again! This is your new world, where you create working software as much as possible, not documentation.

Where a visual designer might have started by making a screen in a graphics editor, this is an opportunity for a front-end engineer to begin.

The engineer opens up a code editor and starts writing some code. Starting with a logged-in version of the homepage, the first thing to create is a list of the jobs this page should be doing. They write some plain text in an HTML document and open it in a web browser to preview what's been done (Figure 8.8).

Version 1 is done! Remember, all that's needed to make a web product is some HTML. Everything else is an optimization. Time to optimize!

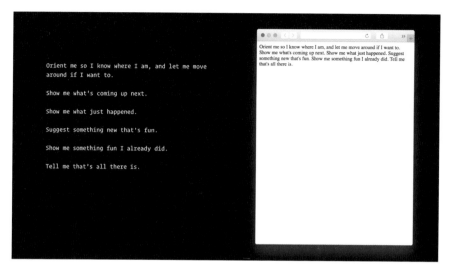

FIGURE 8.8
Plain text rendered in a web browser is a great first version of a web product.

The next steps are really about scaffolding—a fancy way to say some structure is being added to this page, both visually and in code—which is much easier and faster to do in code than in a graphics editor. This is what it looks like to design and decide in the browser. Make each job its own discernible block (Figure 8.9). It's up to the engineer where this is being written, whether it's a blank file in a local code editor, a CodePen, a library creator like Fractal or Pattern Lab, or somewhere else. The important thing is moving quickly and iterating as much as possible.

One pro tip is to shrink the browser window to the smallest width it can go, usually around 320px wide. Working on the smallest screen possible is a major advantage, because the page hierarchy works linearly; no need to worry about columns quite yet. Also, you get all the other benefits of creating mobile-first: it's easy to test with users, the preview environment is responsive by default, and the smaller form factor forces focus as it relates to content creation.

OK, version 2: done!

Now, translate some of the jobs this page has to do into the features and content that actually do that job. You'll see in that first block: "Orient me so I know where I am and let me move around if I want to." An appropriate element for doing all that stuff is a header component, so replace the job phrase with a word or two that describes the actual content going in here (Figure 8.10).

Version 3: done!

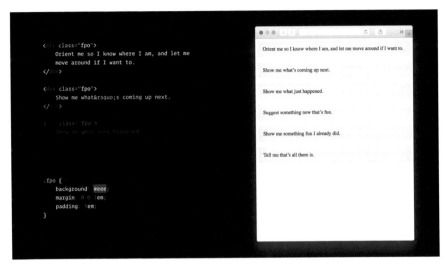

FIGURE 8.9
Add some simple HTML to give structure to the content.

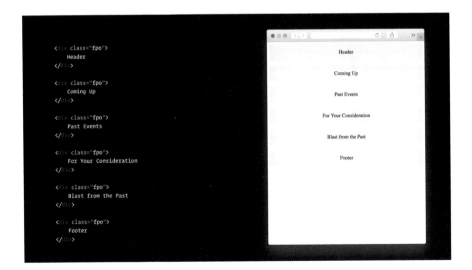

FIGURE 8.10
Replace descriptive content with the name of the component that performs that job.

So far, this is something the front-end engineer has been leading the charge on, but the designer has been paying attention this whole time. At any point along the way, they can revise each other's work. The designer might realize here that "For Your Consideration" and "Blast from the Past" have equal priority so they should always exist side-by-side.

The engineer can take a quick tour to put in a little CSS Grid action—or flexbox, or floats, or any other layout technique of choice—to put that content side-by-side to communicate equal priority. Just like that, version 4 is done (Figure 8.11)!

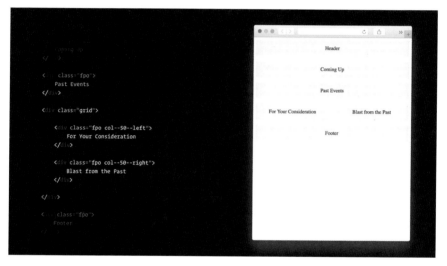

FIGURE 8.11
Structural tweaks can happen early when working in software.

Now, this whole time, the designer wasn't just sitting around watching. The beauty of Hot Potato is that people can be working in parallel. While the engineer sets up the scaffolding, the designer can start playing around with the general art direction. This isn't a UI kit or a component library or really anything finished or too official. This is a thing I like to call an *element collage* (Figure 8.12). Imagine that you took a finished website, printed out all the pages, cut them up, and then spread them all out on the table. An element collage is exactly that, except in reverse. It should be just enough exploration that everyone knows where the designer is headed. This is only a handful of elements, but let's list all the things the engineer might be able to tell about this just from this short visual exploration:

- The name of the app is Trippin'.
- Looks like there's a rounded card motif happening for major pieces of content.
- The typographic palette is a bold sans serif for headlines with a serif italic for some subheads.
- The color palette has at least four major colors in it.

FIGURE 8.12
An element collage for our Trippin' app.

Based on even the little that's currently in that element collage, the engineer could start to set up some design tokens related to things like typography and colors (Figure 8.13). Those tokens may manifest as Sass variables, a JSON file, YAML, or whatever you prefer.

FIGURE 8.13
A configuration file of design decisions in code that the designer can be in charge of.

What's important here is that this becomes a file that the designer is in charge of. That's right designer: you're gonna have to learn some code, or at least code-like concepts. Did you really think we're just going to flip the front-end engineer's world upside-down by making them lead the charge on design, and you could just do what you've always done? Think again! You'll have to learn some new things, like getting familiar with some Sass syntax and maybe even get a local build up and running, but it'll be good for you. Welcome to the party! And don't worry: your engineer can help walk you through it all.

Once this is up and running, these tokens can be tweaked to the designer's heart's content! Rather than the engineer being in charge of getting the design details right, now the designer has the power to do it directly! Say goodbye to redlines forever; just climb into this file to make the changes.

What Do You Need Right Now?

This is my favorite part of Hot Potato, because this is really where it starts rolling. Remember, the front-end engineer is leading the charge, making the software. That means everyone is in service of the engineer. And this is the question everyone should be asking:

Dear Engineer, what do you need right now?

These are the magic words.

As a designer, I'm constantly asking my engineers what they need. My job is in service of theirs. And that's the rest of the team members' jobs, too. We're here solely to help them, because they're the ones closest to the working software.

At this stage, the engineer might say they need some copy for the footer. Copywriter, can you get some copy ready for the footer? If the copywriter is busy, product manager, can you track that down instead? If the product manager's busy, who's not busy right now who can do that?

All Hands on Deck

At this point, it's all hands on deck. Let's pause for a minute to talk about that. When is the only time on a project where it's all hands on deck? Usually, at the end, at crunch time. Everyone's working furiously together, but stressed out, too. If you can move that "all hands on deck" dynamic to way earlier in the project—like at the beginning—you get the same amount of collaboration and help, but without the stress.

Kinda Like This

Engineer, what else do you need? They might say, "I'd love to know what the 'Coming up' section is gonna look like."

The designer replies, "I was thinking it could be a bunch of cards that you can swipe through horizontally." And they could pull their phone out of their pocket and open the App Store. "Yeah, kinda like this middle one" (Figure 8.14). And that will give the engineer enough to go on to prototype. Instead of spending a few hours making a comp, they solved it together in just a few seconds.

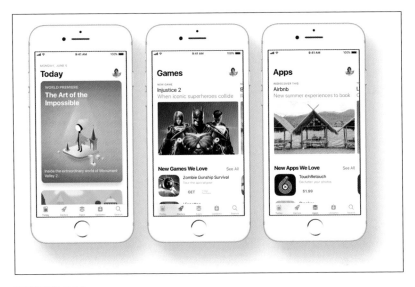

FIGURE 8.14
The Apple App Store acts as a perfect reference for the design and interaction I'd like the Trippin' app to have.

"Kinda like this" is a great phrase to use in a Hot Potato session where you can use references to make sure that you're aligned. References shortcut the time to alignment, as opposed to having to design and build everything from scratch.

Spot Comps

"Engineer, what else do you need right now?"

"I'd love to know what the header looks like," they reply.

The designer may actually have something specific in mind for the hamburger menu button, and they may not have a good reference for it because it's so unique, so "kinda like this" isn't really applicable here. Once all other options have been exhausted, that's the right time for a comp! But not a full comp...just what I like to call a "spot comp," a visual sketch of just one spot on this screen, not the whole screen.

The designer describes what they can in words—"I'm thinking it's the logo on the left and a hamburger icon on the right" so that the engineer can scaffold it—and then the designer goes off to design this specific piece for the next 5–10 minutes while the engineer is building the scaffolding.

Here's what a spot comp looks like in Figure 8.15. It's just one spot of the screen.

While the designer was spending 5–10 minutes spot comping the header, the engineer was dropping in a scrolly-card pattern that can be swiped through (Figure 8.16).

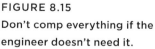

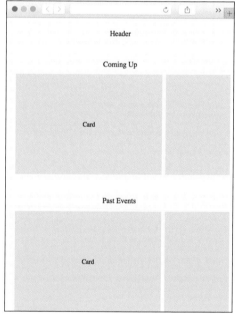

FIGURE 8.15
Don't comp everything if the engineer doesn't need it.

FIGURE 8.16
Scrolly patterns are now added to the page.

The designer drops off a header spot comp. While the engineer is building out the header, the designer might open up those design tokens and start honing the details of the cards, like getting the shape of the card right with the appropriate drop shadow (Figure 8.17) or getting some of the proper typographic styling in there (Figure 8.18).

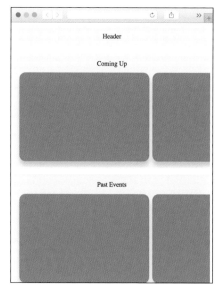

FIGURE 8.17
Colors and rounded corners are added to scrollable cards.

FIGURE 8.18
Proper typography is added.

While the designer was working on those details, the engineer now has the header built out (Figure 8.19).

While the engineer was pulling in the header, the designer started setting up pulling in different colors for different variations of cards (Figure 8.20).

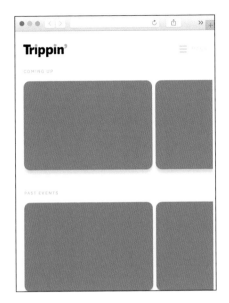

FIGURE 8.19
Header is fully built out.

FIGURE 8.20
Different color cards are added.

I won't take this much further here, but hopefully, you get the idea. After a few hours of this, I hope you can see how a team might collaboratively build out a whole screen. And that may previously be the same amount of time it takes a designer to do a bunch of full static comps in a design tool, and then everything has to start from scratch again when you start the build. With the Hot Potato method, you get everything in the browser as early as possible, and you get the bonus of a responsive working environment while being way closer to making working software with everyone involved in the same process. Hot Potato works best when everyone's working on the same thing at the same time.

One way to best visualize the Hot Potato process is by superimposing a sine wave and an inverted sine wave (Figure 8.21). Hot Potato is about continually coming together to sync up and going apart to have heads-down independent work. The key to this process is keeping the time apart as short as possible. Many teams will let designers go away for one or more weeks before coming back together for scheduled rituals like critique. While that's useful, it's not collaboration; it's designers being independently responsible and not maximizing the amount of help a team can give each other.

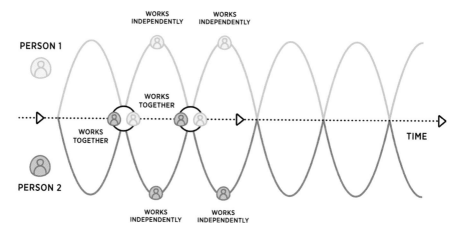

FIGURE 8.21

Hot Potato works best when each party frequently works independently, then together, then independently, and then together.

As teams get more practiced with Hot Potato, the amount of time between coming back together can increase. To the untrained eye, this can look exactly the same as the old waterfall process, but the Hot Potato methodology is crucial to make sure that teams stay connected, and connection is a prerequisite for both collaboration and fruitful design system work.

A Change in Tools Needs a Change in Behavior

Every animal on earth is constrained by its energy budget.

In an article for *Smithsonian Magazine*, editor Jerry Adler proposes that most calories for human beings are burned invisibly through activities like powering the heart, the digestive system, and especially the brain, which silently works to move molecules around within and among its 100 billion cells.[2] A human body at rest devotes roughly one-fifth of its energy to the brain, regardless of whether it is thinking anything useful, or even thinking at all.

2   Jerry Adler, "Why Fire Makes Us Human," *Smithsonian Magazine*, June, 2013, www.smithsonianmag.com/science-nature/why-fire-makes-us-human-72989884/?all

In 2009, Harvard University Professor of Biological Anthropology Richard Wrangham proposed "The Cooking Hypothesis," a theory that our brains became significantly larger than our ancestors' because of cooking. They could spend less time on energy-draining activities like foraging, chewing, and digesting foods because cooking drew out additional nutrients and they had more energy to spend. Larger brains allowed us to process more information, create more dynamic social groups, and adjust to unfamiliar habitats.

And what made this possible? Fire. Legend has it that Prometheus, the son of a Titan, scaled Mount Olympus to steal fire from the workshop of Hephaestus (god of fire and metalworking) and Athena (goddess of war). Prometheus gave the fire to humans, which gave them the power to harness nature for their own benefit and ultimately dominate the natural order. With fire, humans could care for themselves with food and warmth, and they could also forge weapons and wage war. Prometheus's gift of fire acted as a catalyst for the rapid progression of civilization.

When a community gets new powerful tools, their lives can change drastically for the better—if they can fully embrace those new tools into how they live. Prometheus's gift of fire to humans changed the course of humanity forever, because humans did things with it. They cooked food. They migrated. When you get a powerful new tool, you have to change something in your behavior in order to make the most of it.

The biggest pitfall I see with design systems is that designers and engineers still try to work the way they've been working without a design system, even though they may have one now. For example, I'll say to a designer and engineer pair, "Work together on the homepage." This is what they do: the designer goes back to their desk to make a comp of the homepage, and the engineer waits for the designer to make a comp so that they can build it. And they truly believe this is working together. It's not.

Let's look at two examples that hopefully illuminate how different and empowering working together in a truly collaborative way could be.

The Future of Collaborative Work

In 2017, a few designers and engineers at Airbnb conducted an experiment where they classified 150 components in their design system and taught a machine how to recognize them.[3] They built a prototype where they could draw rudimentary shapes on paper, point a camera at the sketch, and a computer translated that low-fidelity sketch into a high-fidelity, coded component in a web browser (Figure 8.22).

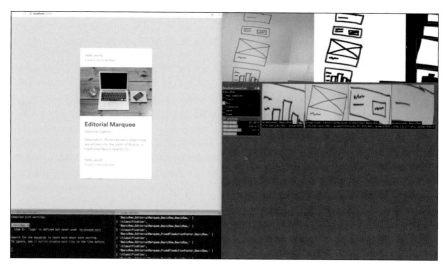

FIGURE 8.22

An experiment by Airbnb about automating UI design through paper sketches.

In 2020, designer Jordan Singer wrote a plug-in for Figma that assessed plain text and translated it into an interface. A designer could type words into a text box: "An app that has a navigation bar with a camera icon, 'Photos' title, and a message icon. A feed of photos with each photo having a user icon, a photo, a heart icon, and a chat bubble icon." And the plug-in will turn that text into a representative interface (Figure 8.23).

---

3   Benjamin Wilkins, "Sketching Interfaces," Airbnb, **https://airbnb.design/ sketching-interfaces/**

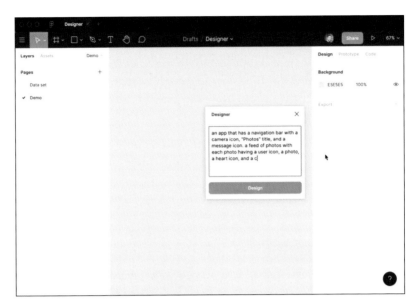

FIGURE 8.23
Jordan Singer's "Designer" plug-in for Figma created interfaces using a text prompt.

I don't know the specific mechanics of how these examples work—they use words like "neural network" and "machine learning" that are above my pay grade right now—but I assume they probably use some natural language processing to somehow tie recognized words and phrases to components in a system.

What's bananas about this is that we as an industry are more willing and able to write software programs that use natural language processing or machine learning to assemble interfaces than we are to sit with a designer or engineer and use these same exact words. Both of these examples assume there's already a system or at least a library in place.

This is how you use a design system when you have it. A designer and engineer can sit down together, and the designer can say, "I'm thinking this could be an app that has a navigation bar with a camera icon, 'Photos' title, and a message icon. A feed of photos with each photo having a user icon, a photo, a heart icon, and a chat bubble icon."

In the previous two examples, the designer "tells" the computer to make something. What's even better about doing this with another person instead of an artificial intelligence is that the engineer could reply, "Ooh, I have a different idea, or a better idea." That kind of conversation is the start of where excellent work comes from, because everyone's invested, and their ideas are represented early on.

Hot Potato Gotchas

The Hot Potato process works wonders, but it does have some gotchas associated with it. Many teams are so used to working the way they have for many years that anything new feels too daunting to take on. Let's address a few common roadblocks and objections to the Hot Potato process.

Start Hot Potato by Sitting Together

Many teams are open to the idea of trying Hot Potato, but they don't exactly know where to begin. It seems overly simplistic, but the best way for designers and engineers to start trying the Hot Potato process is to physically sit together. We've seen many a designer + engineer pair who have worked together for years become enlightened as to how the other works within the first few minutes of sitting together.

If you can't physically sit together, try a video call where the goal is to watch each other work. Push through the initial awkwardness about someone watching you work; try to narrate what you're doing and answer as many questions your partner has, no matter how simple they seem. You may be surprised about how little you know about how your co-workers get their work done and how little they know about how you work. But this is the gateway to tighter and more fruitful collaboration.

Hot Potato for Distributed and Geographically Separate Teams

If you can't work at the same time due to schedules or time zones not lining up, use video to bridge the gap. Record yourself working and send it to your collaborator. Your collaborator can then work alongside your recording while making their own recording. Then continue to pass recordings back and forth. Tools like Loom, Voxer, Marco Polo, and other walkie-talkie- and intercom-like apps help to make asynchronous collaboration feel a bit closer to synchronous collaboration.

Hot Potato for Large Teams

A common concern is that Hot Potato seems viable for a small team of four to six people, but it wouldn't work if you have a hundred-person design or engineering team.

And that's absolutely true: it wouldn't work. The math works against you. If you have a team of three people, there are only three communication points needed between them for the whole team to stay connected. Adding just one more person to the team doubles the number of lines of connection you need between them: for example, a four-person team needs six communication points for the whole team to stay connected (Figure 8.24).

You see how quickly the complexity increases. On a 12-person team, you need 66 lines of connection (Figure 8.25).

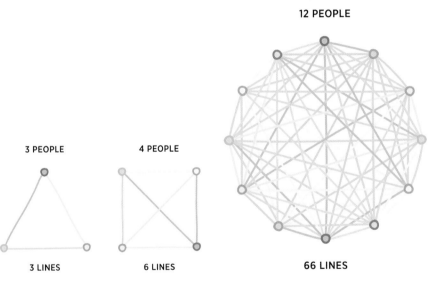

FIGURE 8.24
Adding one more person to a team necessitates three additional connections.

FIGURE 8.25
A 12-person team needs 66 lines of communication to stay connected.

Trying to sustain this is the wrong problem to solve. Instead of trying to navigate the complexity in 66 lines of connection for a 12-person team, break up into two teams of six people that only need 30 connections (Figure 8.26). It's the same number of people, but the scale works against you with a larger team. So, instead of figuring out how to scale this process, try to reduce your scale to capitalize on this process.

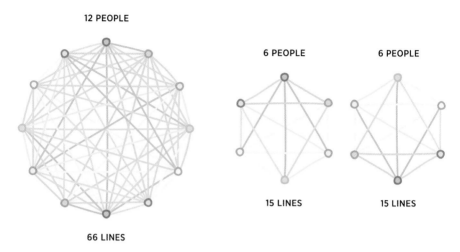

FIGURE 8.26

Splitting a 12-person team into two teams of six people simplifies the communication needed to stay connected.

Resistance to New Workflow

Usually, when I share this kind of Hot Potato, "use your words instead of your hands" process with a new team, engineers get pretty excited and can't wait to try them out. Designers, on the other hand, often put up a bit of resistance. There are usually two different reasons for this. Both are worth addressing, although in very different ways.

Ego

Some designers think they rule the team. This deserves to be dealt with quickly and sternly. There's no room for ego on a collaborative team. It's toxic. If you're a manager, tell your little prima donna that they can shape up or ship out. No matter how much you think you need them, they're probably stifling the rest of the team. Get rid of them, and you'll likely see your team step up to the challenge because now they have room to shine.

Loss of Identity

The second reason I get pushback is much more understandable, because lots of people don't even realize that it's happening. There are usually four types of responses I get from designers that hint at this second reason:

- "There's no way that kind of process would work here."
- "Why do we even need to change things in the first place?!"
- "What if we only try this new process on projects where we have extra time?"
- "Even if this works, it's not like it will make anything better here."

These kinds of sentiments may look familiar to some of you. Respectively, they are signs of the following:

- Denial
- Anger
- Bargaining
- Depression

What are these signs of? Grief. When does one grieve? When they experience loss. And what did they lose? Their identities.

So many designers have their worth tied to the output they create, namely their comps. And for good reason: it's one of the biggest dopamine hits around for a designer to make something quickly and hear the people around them say how awesome it is. Multiply that by the number of years they've been a designer, and it's increasingly more engrained. And all of a sudden, I'm saying to comp less and trust someone else with that job? Now what do they do? Who are they? Who can they become?

If designers are losing their old identities because of this new approach, let's give them new ones. One of my favorite exercises to do when introducing this new kind of working style is that I ask designers to think of their most recent project or two. Regarding those projects, I'll ask them to list all the things they wish they had gotten to do but didn't have time for. Though the conversation might take a little while to get started, I'll eventually start to hear answers like:

- Animating
- Learning a new app (Figma, Framer, etc.)
- Creating custom illustrations

- Learning some code
- Creating a custom icon set
- Writing better documentation
- More accessibility efforts

Finally, it will dawn on them: this isn't writing on the wall. Instead, it's the opposite: this is an opportunity to grow, to further explore their own interests that have previously been unexplored. But the culture needs to exist for designers to feel safe to grow into their new skills.

Questions for Reflection

- How well do you think the Hot Potato process would work at your organization? Make a list of a few teams or even a few pairs or trios that might be the most receptive to giving Hot Potato a try in their next sprint.
- How might future developments like artificial intelligence or automation change your design system process for the better? For the worse?

CHAPTER 9

Success Metrics for a Design System

You can probably already guess the two most common promises of design systems: efficiency and consistency.

Efficiency is straightforward to measure. You can look for things like these indicators to determine if your design system is making your organization more efficient:

- Reduction in design or engineering time from feature teams
- Increase in speed to market
- Reduction in time to perform quality assurance (QA)
- Reduction in bugs filed during the feature creation process

Consistency is a bit more difficult to nail down, but the impact is usually greater if you can do so. For example, a decrease in redundancy within the CSS that designers or engineers are writing may indicate that your digital interfaces are becoming more consistent. You can use tools like CSS Stats[1] to create a benchmark of quantitative data about your CSS and track it over time as more teams use the design system.

You might also track things like reductions in customer complaints or decreases in customer task completion time. There's certainly as much correlation as causation here, but it could be a possible signal that your organization's customers are having a better user experience because of more consistent interface choices.

Ultimately, all of these indicators for efficiency and consistency point to one thing, the holy grail of design system success: adoption. Design system adoption is when feature teams choose to use the design system's components to create their feature or product's interface. The more teams that adopt your design system, the better the experience becomes for your customers, which, in turn, is better for the organization, too.

Unfortunately, adoption is difficult to track. As of the date of this writing, the only viable design system analytics tool I've come across is Omlet,[2] a tool for developers that measures component usage by analyzing your codebase. Otherwise, most of the adoption tracking tools out there have been custom created by and for the teams who have the bandwidth and expertise to build them. The Segment team

---

1 "CSS Stats," https://cssstats.com/

2 "Omlet," https://omlet.dev/

(now part of Twilio) created their own adoption dashboard[3] that tracks precisely which files import a component (Figure 9.1). Graphics editor Figma has its own Library Analytics feature[4] (formerly called *Design System Analytics*[5]) that's exclusive to how designers are using connected components within the Figma environment (Figure 9.2).

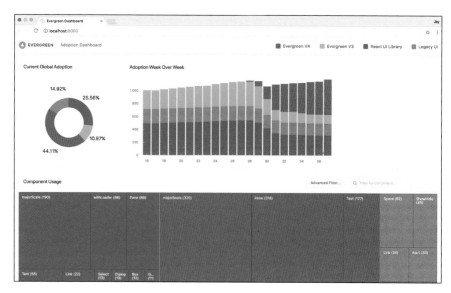

FIGURE 9.1
Segment's custom-built design system adoption tool.

3   Jeroen Ransijn, "How We Drove Adoption of Our Design System," *Segment* (blog), October 16, 2018, **https://segment.com/blog/driving-adoption-of-a-design-system/**

4   "View and Explore Library Analytics," Figma, **https://help.figma.com/hc/en-us/articles/360039238353-View-and-explore-library-analytics**

5   Because it doesn't track code, that version of design system adoption is a little bit different than how this book defines design system products and adoption.

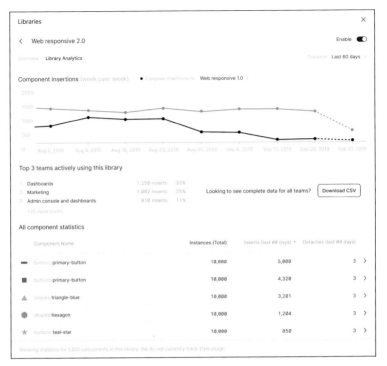

FIGURE 9.2
Figma's Library Analytics tool shows how connected UI kits are.

In his article "Measuring Design System Success," design system consultant Nathan Curtis outlines four topic areas that most design system teams can use to measure how successful their work is:[6]

- Product Adoption
- Operating a Systems Team
- Cultivating a Community
- Monitoring Product Improvement

This is a great starting point, but it's table stakes. It's also what every design system team does, so there's a high-enough likelihood that more than a few of these won't be relevant for your design system initiative.

To really understand how a design system can be impactful in your organization, you'll have to identify some custom success metrics that tie the design system to specific organizational goals more directly.

---

6 Nathan Curtis, "Measuring Design System Success," June 9, 2017, **https://
medium.com/eightshapes-llc/measuring-design-system-success-d0513a93dd96**

DESIGN SYSTEM COVERAGE

How much of any given page of a website should be made up of design system components?

As of this writing, here's the current version of the United Airlines homepage as it stands today (Figure 9.3).

United Airlines' design system is called *Atmos*. Here's the current version of the United Airlines homepage (Figure 9.4), broken down by what *is* an Atmos design system component (highlighted in neon green) and what *is not* (highlighted in pink).

This system isn't based on any insider knowledge of any back-end code or logic. It is purely an analysis of front-end HTML. You can perform the same assessment yourself by inspecting the HTML of this page and looking for any class that starts with atm-, the design system "namespace" for all Atmos components.

Here are all the different kinds of components that can—and often do—live together on one page:

- Components that come straight out of the design system
- Components that are custom built for this page or a specific feature on this page
- Components that are forked or duplicated versions of what also lives in the design system

continues

FIGURE 9.3

The United Airlines homepage, made up of many different kinds of components.

- Components that started here where an abstracted version eventually ended up in the design system
- Components from the design system whose styles are being augmented or overwritten
- Design system components nested inside of nondesign system containers
- Custom components nested inside of design system containers

What variety! And that's OK! This is the reality of enterprise product design at scale. It reflects the nature of parallel roadmaps, design system team resourcing and bandwidth, business priorities, and many more factors.

Some organizations seem to strive for an ideal that, once a design system exists, everything in an interface can and should be built with it. Not only is that an unrealistic goal for most enterprises, but it can often be a toxic mindset to think that anything less than 100% coverage is a misuse of a design system at best or an utter failure at worst.

Use the Pareto principle—often known as the "80/20 rule"—to set an actionable target for teams: aim for up to 80% of any given page to be made of design system components and leave room for about 20% of the page to be custom. That remaining 20% is where the invention and innovation can happen. I recently heard an anecdote from a design system team who reported that they spent only 20% of their sprint

FIGURE 9.4

The United Airlines homepage is shown classified with Atmos and non-Atmos components.

time creating 80% of their pages with the design system, which then freed up 80% of the sprint time to work on the 20% of custom functionality that really made the experience sing. This is exactly the kind of innovation that design systems should enable!

One nuance to add to this 80/20 rule for page makeup is that 80% is the maximum target, not the starting point. So, what's a good starting target for design system coverage on a page?

Use 10% as a starting point, with a plan to work up to 80% eventually, likely over the course of a year or two. Coincidentally, the United Airlines home-page shows this in action. Of eight major sections of the page—admittedly a touch oversimplified for the purposes of this example—one major section (12.5%) is powered by the design system.

But even 10% is too ambitious sometimes. For a more attainable starting point, try to get one component adopted by a few feature teams simul-taneously. It seems trivial, but there's a mountain of work that goes into implementing one component—especially the first component—into a codebase that will eventually make its way to production. The effort from zero adopted components to one is the steepest, and there's a long tail of decreasing effort from there (Figure 9.5).

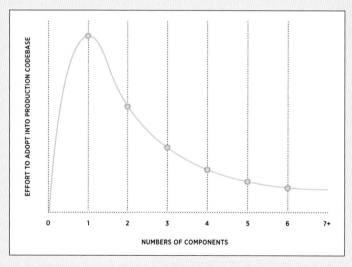

FIGURE 9.5
It's most difficult to get the first component implemented.

continues

For teams where even one component is too much to take on, getting *anything* adopted is a good first step. I often suggest a plain neon green box, like a <div> with a width, height, and background color. You might think I'm joking, but I'm not! Once the hurdle of getting something from one codebase imported into another is crossed, it's easier to iterate into more, better, and higher quality components than it is to try and create a perfect one the first time around.

Don't worry if you aren't creating everything with your design system! Be kind to yourself, your colleagues, and your teams. Give yourself permission to start with just one component, or even just one neon green box. If you can make that happen, it's all downhill from there!

Identifying Custom Success Metrics

In his book, *Change by Design*,[7] executive chair of design firm IDEO Tim Brown discussed helping people articulate their needs. He wrote, "The easiest thing about the search for insight...is that it's everywhere and it's free."

There are many different methodologies you can use to get insight on the work of identifying custom success metrics that lies ahead. In her book, *How to Make Sense of Any Mess*,[8] information architect Abby Covert suggested a few questions you can ask about in your search for insight:

- Why does this work need to be done?
- Why is change needed?
- Why do those changes matter?
- Why should other people care?
- Why hasn't this been tackled correctly?
- Why will this time be different?

---

7 Tim Brown, *Change by Design* (New York: HarperBusiness, 2009).

8 Abby Covert, *How to Make Sense of Any Mess* (Self-published, 2014).

In his book, *Interviewing Users*,[9, 10] user researcher Steve Portigal suggested themes that are ripe for insight exploration:

- Sequence
- Quantity
- Exceptions
- Complete list
- Relationships
- Organizational structure
- Clarification
- Native language
- Emotional cues
- Process
- Time

Regardless of the specific line of questioning, talk to about 30 people. That's a large enough subset to give you a mountain of insight about what's important to the organization as a whole.

Now that you have a broad view of all or most of the things that are important to everyone, it's time to rank them.

Use the KJ Method to Determine Priorities

Ethnographer Jiro Kawakita pioneered the idea of affinity mapping, which is the idea of grouping similar data to simplify the process of deciding what matters most. Nicknamed the *KJ Method* for its founder, make this technique a regular go-to for creating organizationally relevant success metrics for your design system:

1. Talk to 30 individuals and record their beliefs about what's important to a design system effort. (Alternatively, you could collect this data by asking people to submit answers through a digital survey.)
2. Group items together that seem related and name the group.
3. Bring all of the people that you originally talked to together and share the groups of priorities with them.

---

9   Steve Portigal, *Interviewing Users*, 2nd Edition (New York: Rosenfeld Media, 2023).

10 Another Rosenfeld Media cross-sell unlocked! We Rosenfeld authors secretly have a royalty pool going. We're like the Illuminati of user experience books, arguably the least popular of all Illuminati chapters.

4. Give each participant three votes and ask them to choose their top three priorities.

When done well, you can easily start to see what everyone believes success looks like. A shared idea of success is a crucial ingredient in establishing a design system practice that lasts.

A Framework to Measure Success

There are many different measurement frameworks for figuring out how to track the progress of work:

- You can define service-level agreements (SLAs) to memorialize understandings about priorities and responsibilities.
- You can use key performance indicators (KPIs) and operational performance indicators (OPIs) to focus on the key targets that make the biggest impact on realizing your organization's high-level strategy.
- You can employ the Jobs-to-Be-Done framework to define and focus relentlessly on your customers' needs.
- You can make hard choices using Top Tasks Management to center the five or fewer tasks that matter most to your customers.
- You can define (objectives and key results) (OKRs) to keep your teams constantly aimed at the bull's-eye.

Saying too much more about each methodology is a bit beyond the scope of this book, but they're all worth considering and researching further.

My favorite is OKRs, so let's look at how you might define some custom ones for your design system.

Defining Success with OKRs (Objectives and Key Results)

Venture capitalist John Doerr presented the idea of OKRs to Google's leadership in 1999 when they were less than a year old, and they've been in use ever since. OKRs were originally implemented at Intel in the 1970s. Now, companies like Google, LinkedIn, Zynga, Sears, Oracle, and Twitter are just a handful of organizations that use OKRs to drive their businesses.

OKRs stand for *objectives and key results*, and both parts are necessary in a framework for keeping teams on track.

- An *objective* is a statement that is vague, ambitious, and somewhat comfortable. Objectives usually start with a verb.

- A *key result* is a measurable statement that is set and evaluated quarterly. Key results usually contain a number.

Objectives are relatively easy to unearth. In fact, all of the groups' names you just created in the KJ Method serve as perfect objectives, as they're probably all vague, ambitious, and somewhat comfortable.

The next question to answer is, "How will we know that we're making progress?" The evaluation scale is the main reason I prefer the OKR framework above the others. OKRs aren't goals or targets. They're not about achieving a goal; they're about making progress. You're not grading your results; instead, you're evaluating your progress. The way you evaluate key results is on a scale from 0–10 (or 0–100, if you prefer, which I do). The aim for any given key result is somewhere from 60 to 80. Why not 100? Well, imagine you hit 100. It would be easy to question whether you sandbagged that key result—that is, you set a key result that you knew you'd hit. Which begs the question: Were you not being ambitious enough? A target score of 60–80 means that you're probably doing something a bit ambitious and that your intention is to do pretty well against that ambitious thing. That's a great mindset for a design system team—or any team—to have.

Of course, this cuts both ways. If you get a 0 on a key result, you were probably being too ambitious to the point where it was unrealistic. Be kind to yourself. OKRs provide a wide playing field to experience some wins in the context of work that can push you…a good balance.

The first questions I often get when creating key results with teams are, "Where do we get the numbers from? How do we know if we're trying to improve or decrease a metric by 1% or 42% or 75%?"

Admittedly, the first time you create OKRs, you will likely be wildly off. That's OK! It's the first time you're doing it! You don't have to be perfect. Remember: the great thing about OKRs is that they're not about hitting a target; they're about measuring progress. Think about it this way: the first time you set OKRs will be the most difficult and probably the worst. You're establishing a benchmark. The next time (next quarter), it will be slightly less difficult and a little less bad. One day, a few quarters from now, setting OKRs will start to feel normal and maybe even easy. Said differently, the point of this quarter's OKRs is that you'll have a better starting point for next quarter's OKRs.

Now you've accepted that you don't have to be perfect about nailing your first set of OKRs. Still, you have to start somewhere, right? So, do you just pick a number out of a hat?

There's a branch of psychology called *psychophysics*, which investigates the relationship between physical stimuli and the sensations and perceptions they produce. In psychophysics, they talk a lot about the *just noticeable difference* (JND), which says time intervals are prone to be between 7% to 18% on average for periods with a duration of less than 30 seconds. That means for someone to perceive, "Hey, that was faster/better/slower/worse," the difference has to be at least 7–18%. Because of the JND, my first key results are generally looking for a 15%–20% change (increase or decrease) in some element.

Make OKRs Matter by Scheduling Time to Track Them

It's not enough to simply set good OKRs. After you've identified them, you have to make them matter by building a practice around them.

Add three events to your calendar:

- **Every Friday:** Set aside an hour to look at the data for all of your key results to record what's changed.

- **Every Monday:** Set aside an hour to write an update to your fellow design team members to make progress—or the lack of it—visible. Make this message applicable at the ground level that everyone's working on. Spend time in this message focusing more on key results rather than objectives, especially on what each team member can do or try to influence the key results in the direction you want to see them go.

- **On the last Friday of each month:** Draft a message to all the people you initially interviewed and report what you've learned in the previous four weeks of tracking. Keep this message high-level by focusing more on the objectives than the key results—the opposite weighting of the message you send to the team each week.

There are a few tools that can automate key result tracking, but I'd suggest you do it manually for the first 2–4 quarters of implementing OKRs. The more intimately familiar you are with the data, how it's being collected, and how much it can be influenced, the better story you'll be able to tell around how your design system is contributing to the company's overall goals.

SUCCESS METRICS FOR THE GENERAL CONFERENCE OF SEVENTH-DAY ADVENTISTS: A CASE STUDY

A few years ago, my team at SuperFriendly and I worked on a project for the General Conference of Seventh-day Adventists to create a design system for them. The Seventh-day Adventist (SDA) church is a centralized, global organization. They have many suborganizations: over 70,000 churches worldwide organized into 13 world divisions; 63 publishing houses offering publications in over 350 languages; over 7,500 primary schools; 15 media centers; and disaster relief in 130 countries.

To better understand what people needed from the new design system, we talked to different kinds of people. We talked to people who build websites for any of the suborganizations, from web professionals in charge of multiple sites to church secretaries learning WordPress for the first time to publish the weekly service bulletin online. We talked to people who visited SDA websites both regularly and nonregularly. We talked to people who worked at the General Conference about what the organization needed from a new design system.

Our script for these conversations was simple. In general, we asked people about themselves. What do they do as part of their normal routines? What do they love about it? What do they wish they could change? Simple questions like these provoked 30–60 minutes of interesting conversations that served as great fodder for the needs the design system had to meet.

For the SDA, we organized all of the insights into these common themes and objectives. After employing the KJ Method, it was easy to visualize where consensus lay: at the highest concentration of Post-its (Figure 9.6).

FIGURE 9.6
A voting session quickly surfaced the themes most and least important to everyone in the room.

continues

The three top priorities became our objectives:

- Create a foundational, deeply rooted design system.
- Allow for customization and individuality.
- Involve the community in creation and adoption.

Here is the first quarter of OKRs we set up for the new Adventist Living Pattern System (ALPS):

Objective: Create a foundational, deeply rooted design system.

Key Results:

1. 1,800 Adventist websites (15% of the 12,000 sites in the Seventh-day Adventist network) make obvious use of ALPS.

2. 57 websites made by the General Conference (50% of the 114 websites created directly by the General Conference) make obvious use of ALPS.

3. The first websites built in these languages using ALPS report 0 issues when building:

    a. Mandarin
    b. Spanish
    c. English
    d. Hindi/Urdu
    e. Arabic
    f. Portuguese
    g. Bengali
    h. Russian
    i. Japanese
    j. Punjabi
    k. German
    l. French

Objective: Allow for customization and individuality.

Key Results:

1. A trained person can build a site with ALPS in two days or less.

2. 2,400 Adventist websites (20% of the 12,000 websites in the network) use one of the default color preset options (Figure 9.7).

Objective: Involve the community in creation and adoption.

Key Results:

1. Eighteen unions (30% of the organization) register in our feedback program.

2. Three ideas originating from the community not included in the initial launch of ALPS have been adopted.

3. ALPS is adopted by three customers who weren't part of the initial round of customer interviews or any feedback program.

FIGURE 9.7

ALPS contained many different color themes for constituents to choose from that expressed their individuality.

What I absolutely love about these OKRs is how specific they are to the Adventist Church and ALPS. They push beyond default and generic metrics of adoption and focus on change that's meaningful for the mission of the organization.

People Succeed, Not Systems

The big epiphany in creating meaningful success metrics for your design system really occurs when you start looking for how the people who make and use the design system succeed, not the system itself. Most design system teams start by declaring key results like "15% increase in adoption of form components" when a better focus would be "Landing Pages teams (teams that use forms) complete their work one week faster." Certainly, two sides of the same coin, but the latter opens up a myriad of possibilities for design system strategy by focusing on how the people using the design system succeed.

Here are a few areas to look for where people can succeed.

Keep Your Team Motivated with Autonomy, Mastery, and Purpose

The early days of the web were a mix of experiments ranging from news websites to forums to comics to personal expression and much more. As the web evolved, more people and corporations started to run their businesses on the internet. The Interactive Advertising Bureau reported that in 2020, the internet contributed $2.45 trillion (over 11%) to the United States' GDP.[11] The web is now Serious Business.™

As a result, the need to track and report useful quantitative data that helps businesses grow is high. But I think the pendulum has swung a little too far. As an industry, I think we now tend to overprioritize the quantitative. We want dashboards, analytics tools, and hard metrics. That's good. It's a correction to an era where we just "felt it all out." But I think it may be an overcorrection.

In his book, *Drive*, Daniel Pink described a framework for what drives people and what motivates them:

- **Autonomy:** The desire to direct our own lives
- **Mastery:** The urge to become better at something that matters
- **Purpose:** The yearning to contribute and be part of a cause greater and more enduring than ourselves

---

11 "Study Finds Internet Economy Grew Seven Times Faster Than Total U.S. Economy, Created over 7 Million Jobs in the Last Four Years," October 18, 2021, www.iab.com/news/study-finds-internet-economy-grew-seven-times-faster/

What does this have to do with design systems? Well, nothing in particular. But also…everything! The job of a design system is to take care of the mundane, so that everyone on the team can have some amount of autonomy, mastery, and purpose. Sometimes, designers in particular see a design system itself as a direct threat to their autonomy because a system of reusable elements removes the point that previously held the most autonomy for designers: the creation process.

To combat that, make a list of all the things your team promises to do "if we have extra time at the end." You know—it's the list of stuff that never gets done. Usual suspects on this list typically include activities with the words "custom" or "more" or "trying out" in them: art-directing a custom photo shoot, more animation, trying out new tools, etc. Assure your team that their continued investment in design success means they get to do more of the things on this list.

Design Systems as Relief

Earlier in the chapter, I outlined efficiency and consistency as some of the most typical promises of a design system, but I think there's a much more important one that often gets overlooked: The most impactful promise of a design system should be as a *relief* to the people who use it. Because our industry's collective work can contribute two freakin' trillion dollars to a country's GDP, many of our jobs now come with a dose of intense pressure. Honestly, most of it is undue. It's not that deep; no one's gonna die if you mess up. (For those of you who work on design systems for life-or-death digital products, we thank you for your service.) For all the rest of you, be kinder to yourselves and your teams by relieving some of that pressure.

Efficiency is a good thing, but you don't always have to use that efficiency to get *more* work done. Efficiency should allow you to rest more sometimes. Instead of "do more in the same amount of time," what about "do the same amount in a shorter amount of time and take more breaks?"

Relief is even more difficult to measure than efficiency and consistency, but its impact is more critical. Some areas to observe whether your design system is truly a relief:

- **Turnover:** Is turnover lower for those who work on or use the design system than those who don't?
- **Job satisfaction:** Do the people who work on or use the design system enjoy their jobs more than those who don't? In the results

of their latest "How We Document" survey, the team at design system documentation tool zeroheight starts to draw some correlations between design system work and job satisfaction.[12]

- **Creativity and innovation:** Using your organization's standards for innovation, are people and teams who have direct ties to the design system being more creative and innovative than people and teams who don't?

- **Team engagement and psychological safety:** Are people and teams who have direct ties to the design system more engaged and supportive than people and teams who don't?

Here are some examples of key results that really test whether your design system is living up to its fullest potential:

- Increase retention on [team that has the highest turnover] by 15%.
- Receive five new feature proposals from teams that have used the design system.
- 15% increase in positive and supportive language in design critiques.

Invest in Both Your Stables and Volatiles

Michael Lopp was a former engineering manager at Apple before moving on to run engineering at Pinterest and now Slack. Over the last decade, I have yet to find an article that better describes the product creation narrative than his article "Stables and Volatiles."[13] In it, he thinks about how engineering teams can get to a v1 of a piece of software and what happens shortly after. He says, "The birth of 1.0 initiates a split of the development team into two groups: Stables and Volatiles." The article goes into depth about the specific characteristics of both, but generally:

- *Stables* tend to rely on process for predictability and measurability and are known for being reliable and calm.

- *Volatiles* don't often build beautiful or stable things, but they do build a lot, and they tend to leave a trail of disruption in their wake.

---

12 Luke Murphy, "What Makes a Happy Design System Team?" *zeroheight* (blog), May 10, 2022, **https://zeroheight.com/blog/what-makes-a-happy-design-system-team/**

13 Michael Lopp, "Stables and Volatiles," November 14, 2012, **https://randsinrepose.com/archives/stables-and-volatiles/**

Lopp concluded the article by saying, "I believe a healthy company that wants to continue to grow and invent needs to equally invest in both their Stables and their Volatiles."

Applying this approach to a design system fits perfectly. Yes, a major benefit of a design system is creating efficiency by reuse. But even if you can build everything you dream of with your design system, don't. Sure, it will count as success for your Stables, but say goodbye to your Volatiles. A design system is a product, and like any good product team, some people can work on the settled solutions while others can venture out, seeking the new.

Favor Incentive over Punishment

Charlie Munger is the vice chairman of Berkshire Hathaway, the financial conglomerate controlled by Warren Buffett. In a university commencement speech, he once said, "Punishment works best to prevent actions whereas incentives work best to encourage them."

People are often asked to do new things under fear of punishment. That doesn't make sense. It works sometimes, but it's confusing. Teams get told, "You have a year to migrate to the new tech stack." And the subtext is, "Or else something bad will happen." Right? Per Munger's quote here, the threat of punishment is more likely to get people to *stop* doing something rather than get them to *start* doing something, like learning a new technology or adopting a new tool like a design system.

A common mantra across design system teams is, "Make the right to do the easiest thing to do." In 2016, the design and engineering teams at United Airlines were given a year to migrate off of the old .NET tech stack, as well as get their UI in line with the new rebrand. They used that mandate as the primary value proposition of adopting their new Atmos design system, so much so that it was the first line of text on the reference site homepage (Figure 9.8): "Atmos is the easiest way to bring the new United Airlines visual language and React tech stack to your application."

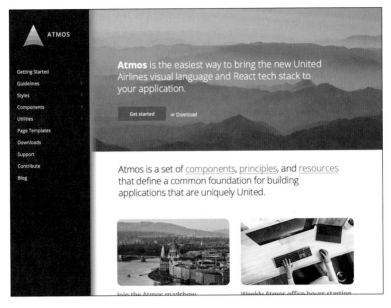

FIGURE 9.8
The first line of the Atmos reference site was designed to signal that it was the easiest way to do the right thing.

Align Goals to Connect an Organization

A design system team's goal is often not the same as a product team's goal. The design system team's goal is usually adoption of the design system. The product team's goals are often some form of customer value.

When there's tension between a design system team's goals and a product team's goals, which one do you prioritize? There's an easy answer: the product team's. A design system team is a service team. The design system team should tie their goals to product team's goals. That way, as the product team wins, the design system team wins, too, as a result.

In Chapter 1, "Why Design Systems?," I defined design systems as a mechanism for connecting an organization. So far, I've described the technical connections a design system makes through code and workflow. Even more powerful, design systems can kick-start a connection between teams that have similar and overlapping goals.

Focus your design system work on specifically supporting how your organization creates customer value, and you'll get your goal—design system adoption—for free.

Questions for Reflection

- How can you write or rewrite your team's OKRs with a specific focus and tie them to how your organization creates customer value?

- Can you identify the specific ways that people on your team get autonomy, mastery, and purpose?

- Who on your team is a Stable and who is a Volatile? Is everyone working on things that align with their personality type?

- Do you or your managers use incentive or fear of punishment to drive your team? Are you trying to get them to stop doing existing things or start doing new things?

CHAPTER 10

Evangelism Never Stops

In the suburbs of Philadelphia, there's a store called Andy's Brick Shop. It's a store full of Legos, and it's a perfect analogy for what an ideal experience of interacting with a design system should be like.

The entrance of the store features a showcase of all the coolest—and most expensive—things people have made with Legos, for sale already assembled. The first things you see are a $360 Star Wars Y-wing (Figure 10.1), a $368 Star Wars Snowspeeder (Figure 10.2), a $100 Space Shuttle Orbiter (Figure 10.3), and an $80 assembled Millennium Falcon (Figure 10.4).

FIGURE 10.1
A $360 Star Wars Y-wing.

FIGURE 10.2
A $368 Star Wars Snowspeeder.

FIGURE 10.3
A $100 Space Shuttle Orbiter.

FIGURE 10.4
An $80 assembled Millennium Falcon.

As you get past the higher-end assembled pieces, you see some lower-value assembled pieces, like these $8 houses and storefronts (Figure 10.5).

Toward the middle of the store lining the walls are different "universes" that show assembled sets, from Star Wars (Figure 10.6) to Tolkien's Middle Earth (Figure 10.7) to DC and Marvel Comics (Figure 10.8), and more.

FIGURE 10.5
$8 houses and storefronts.

FIGURE 10.6
The Lego Star Wars universe.

FIGURE 10.7
The Lego Middle Earth universe.

FIGURE 10.8
The Lego DC and Marvel universes.

As you move past different "universes," you start to see collections by type instead of by theme. This is where you'll find armies of Chewbaccas (Figure 10.9), Batmen (Figure 10.10), C-3POs (Figure 10.11), Supermen (Figure 10.12), and more.

FIGURE 10.9
Lego Chewbaccas.

FIGURE 10.10
Lego Batmen.

FIGURE 10.11
Lego C-3POs.

FIGURE 10.12
Lego Supermen.

Further back in the store, you'll find the organization gets more granular, as parts are separated into types like gears, connectors, sprockets, flames, pots, wheels, and more (Figure 10.13).

There's even a whole section of heads (Figure 10.14). Lots and lots of heads (Figure 10.15).

FIGURE 10.13
Legos, organized by type.

FIGURE 10.14
Heads.

FIGURE 10.15
Lots of Lego heads.

Farther back still, once you pass the categories of parts, you'll find parts not organized into categories (Figure 10.16). There are big bins of random assortments. Some of these parts will one day be categorized, while others won't be.

Lastly, at the very back of the store, there's a trash bin for fake legos (Figure 10.17). They exist. Andy's Brick Shop acknowledges it and makes room for it while still letting you know that they're different from everything else you find in the store.

FIGURE 10.16
Unorganized Legos.

FIGURE 10.17
A trash bin for fake legos.

Here's the full view of the store (Figure 10.18). They occasionally host classes and meetups where enthusiasts can convene, learn from each other, and just play! What an amazing place!

FIGURE 10.18
Andy's Brick Shop, in all its full glory.

Lay Out Your Design System like a Store

Most design systems could learn a lot from the way Andy's Brick Shop engages its customers and community. In fact, many design system teams do it completely opposite, to their detriment.

Most of the popular, public design system reference sites lead with the least compelling parts first—components. It's not that components aren't important; they're crucial to a design system. But highlighting components first misses the opportunity to present what's even more appealing to the audience of designers and engineers and product managers that could use the system. It's the same idea behind the mainstream marketing mantra, "Nobody wants a quarter-inch drill. They want a quarter-inch hole." The biggest mistake most public design system reference sites make is that they don't lead with the *results* that can come from using the design system (Figure 10.19).[1]

---

1 "Atlassian Design System," https://atlassian.design/

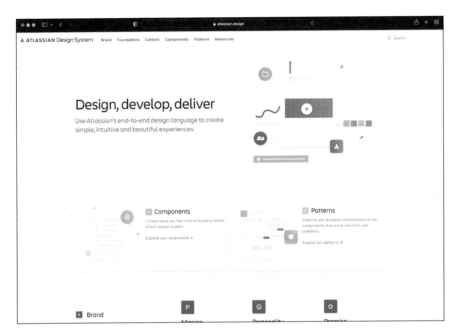

FIGURE 10.19
Though beautiful and functional, the Atlassian Design System reference site misses a bigger opportunity by leading with components and patterns.

Highlighting components first would be like Andy's Brick Shop putting a bin of heads at the front of the store. It would be an odd signal to send to customers, to communicate that this is just a store where you can find parts instead of a store where you can immerse yourself in universes you love and expand your ability to play to match your imagination. Of course, it is a store where you can find parts, but the context and the opportunity are much larger.

The first things people should see when they come to a reference site are examples of the kinds of things that could be made with that design system. That may be an odd thought if you're thinking about a reference site as a technical documentation site. It is, but only partially. Don't forget that a reference site is a marketing site, too.

The Material Design website would be much more powerful if it led with how consistent interfaces between products like Gmail, Search, and Maps make Google users more productive. What a statement it would be for Atlassian to show their design system implemented in tools like Trello and Jira and Bitbucket as a primary driver for how teams get their work done. Putting your organization's equivalent of the Millennium Falcon at the front of the store makes more people walk in (Figure 10.20).[2]

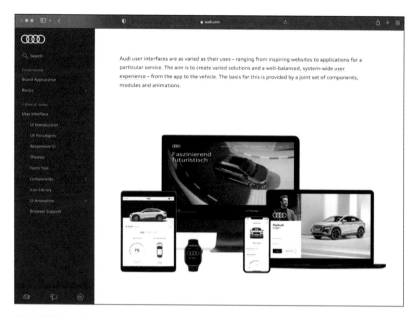

FIGURE 10.20
Audi's user interface guide is one of the few that prominently highlight the kinds of products that can be made with it.

Make Your Design System About Its Users

Another big reason to focus more on the products that can be made with the system than the parts that make it up is that it signals that the people using the system are as important—if not more—than the people making the system. Components are the work of the design system team, but products are the work of feature teams. If products are nowhere to be found on design system reference sites, the idea that digital products can be made from a combination of the components gets lost. At that point, it's just a portfolio site for the design system team.

---

2 "UI Introduction," Audi, **www.audi.com/ci/en/guides/user-interface/introduction.html**

Focusing on end results also opens doors to many additional oppor-tunities. Astro is the design system for the United States Space Force, and they highlight a few examples of the kinds of products that can be—and have been—made with the system (Figure 10.21).

FIGURE 10.21

The GRM Dashboard, one example of a real product that has been made with the Astro Design System.

But it doesn't stop there. The team there uses the opportunity to show how the page has been constructed, breaking down the anatomy of the page and the components used (Figure 10.22).

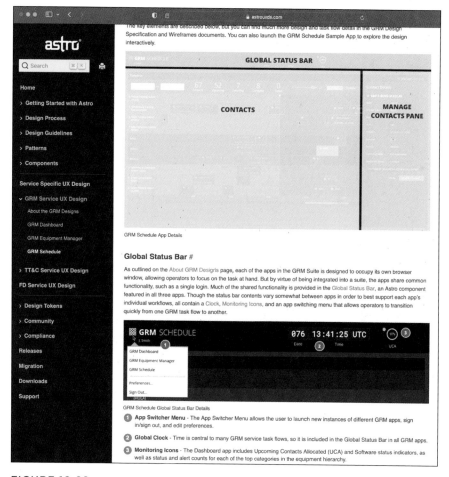

FIGURE 10.22
A breakdown of the GRM Dashboard product.

They link to a live demo of the application so you can see for yourself how the components all work together (Figure 10.23).

FIGURE 10.23
The real GRM product.

As if that wasn't enough, they link to a Bitbucket repository (Figure 10.24) so that you can see the source code behind this application.

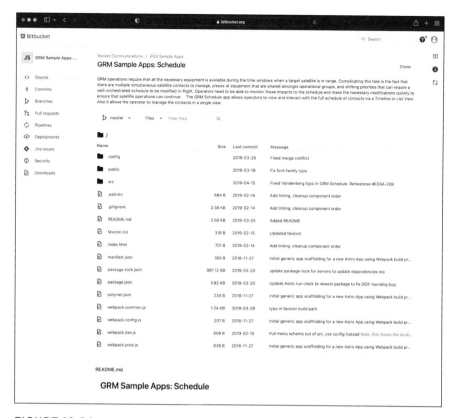

FIGURE 10.24
The Bitbucket repository for the GRM product so you can see its source code.

This is a design system at its zenith. It's more than plug-and-play components. It's more than assembling parts into a layout. It's more than documentation as a dry instruction manual. It's a whole eco-system that describes a way of doing things, shows you examples as starting points, and gives you the ingredients to try it yourself.

Don't miss the chance to give the users of your design system every advantage to make their jobs easier, so that they can give their customers a chance to make their lives easier. It's a cycle that keeps on giving, but it starts with reminding your design system customers that using your design system is going to somehow improve their lives and that they are a crucial part of that formula. Sure, they'll find components here, but the context of it is to make their work lives easier, faster, and overall better somehow.

Otherwise, your design system is just a bin of heads.

Questions for Reflection

- What's your version of "The Millennium Falcon" in your design system? How can you make it the first thing showcased when someone comes in contact with your design system?

- What pieces of instructional documentation can you instead replace with stories, examples, and templates?

I once worked with a company that went through a rebranding effort. The rebrand was simple: changing all of their yellow buttons to purple buttons. They estimated the effort to be around 11 months of work, to the tune of about $10 million.

This company managed hundreds of websites and applications across many different platforms, and each one was built from scratch by a different team using different approaches.

This rebrand should have taken four weeks maximum: one day to implement the color change in one place and four weeks to test and make sure they didn't break anything important. But they didn't have a system that connected all of the buttons to one canonical source. Instead, they spent the amount of time and money it takes to put on a Broadway show.

After reading this book, you have the knowledge to avoid this situation for your team or company. Here are the four biggest lessons I hope you take with you:

- Real organizational value lies in truly connected design systems.
- Pilots are the easiest way to make a design system that's kindest for the teams making it and using it.
- True collaboration takes the most advantage of the promises of a great design system.
- You can serve people well if you understand what drives them.

French author Antoine de Saint-Exupéry once wrote about a man who wanted to build a seaworthy vessel. This man was able to rally a group of friends to perform all of the tasks needed to build the said vessel. How? This popular motivational quote is said to have emerged from that story:

> If you wish to build a ship, do not divide the men into teams and send them to the forest to cut wood.
>
> Instead, teach them to long for the vast and endless sea.

The state of the world is increasingly alarming. Pandemics and recessions and layoffs make people anxious for their livelihoods, so the least we can do for some people is make work as unremarkable as possible. For those who work in tech, establishing and sustaining design systems practices are a great way to do that.

As designers, engineers, and product people—and especially if you're a manager or a leader—your primary job isn't to increase efficiency and drive innovative results. It's to take care of the people you work with. Help them. Protect them. Make their work easy. Inspire them. Excite them. Challenge them. Make work a place of relief for them.

I wrote this book to help you understand design systems more intimately, which I hope it did. But what's the point of that? Design systems aren't "the vast and endless sea." Design systems are the ship. The vast and endless sea is a world where our work is more interesting, more safe, and more fun, and generally happier. Because that's the stuff that can make the world just a little bit better for everyone.

as ecosystems, 12, 54

emergent, 91–93, 147–148

how to use, compared with component libraries, 37–39

minimum viable, 90–91

public, 30–32, 199–201

as relief, 187–188

succeeding in career path of, 7–10

success with three-legged stools (Engineering, Product, and Design), 128–129

design systems, kinds of, 14–21

as brand identities and visual languages, 14–15

as digital products, 17–18

as a practice, 20–21

as a process, 19

as projects, 15

as a service, 20

as tools and templates, 15–16

design systems, parts of, 24–34

component library, 26–29

design tokens, 32–33

digital products (websites and applications), 33–34

guidelines, 29–30

reference website, 30–32

UI (user interface), 25–26

design tokens, 32–33

designers

collaborative work with engineers, 151–161

front-end engineers as, 120, 121–125

resistance to Hot Potato workflow, 167–169

DesignOps (design operations), 132–136

defined, 132

design system teams in, 20

establishing and growing, 136

importance of, 135

as producers/project managers, 131

relationship with design systems, 133–134

skills for professionals, 134

TeamOps and ProductOps, 134, 136

digital products. *See* products, digital

display components vs. content components, 71–77

diversity in teams, 122–123

Do Scale (McKeown), 78

documentation

design system guidelines, 29

prioritization over software, 114–115

during product design cycle, 105–107

public reference websites, 30–32

Doerr, John, 180

downloading files, 32, 36, 37

Drive (Pink), 186

E

ecosystem engineers, 127–128

ecosystems, design systems as, 12, 54

efficiency, measurement of, 172, 187

element collage, 154–155

emergent design systems, 91–93, 147–148

emergent strategies, 91, 103

energy budgets, of humans and animals, 161

Engineering organization

hierarchy in org chart, 137–139

as one leg of three-legged stool, 128–129

engineers. *See also* front-end engineering

collaborative work with designers, 151–161

software prioritization over documentation, 114–115

T hank you, God, for lining up the experiences and moments that gave me enough knowledge and ability to write a book like this.

Thank you to my wife Emily and daughters Sidda and Charlie for all your support while I did something as silly and exciting and draining and energizing and daring and audacious and humbling as writing a book.

Thank you to the entire Rosenfeld Media crew. Lou Rosenfeld: this book would not have happened without you. Thank you for believing in me enough to let me fly the Rosenfeld flag behind my words. I appreciate the wrestling matches we had that made our work together and our relationship stronger. Marta Justak: we hit it off in our first conversation with our shared love of serial commas. Thank you for pushing me to write the book that I wanted to write and helping me to avoid too many gerunds. Kevin Hoffman: thanks for introducing me to Lou. Without that connection, this book wouldn't have existed.

To my reviewers, Jesse Gardner and Alex Rice, thank you for the thoughtful and superb comments on my drafts. Many sections of this book exist because of you, and readers were also spared many tragedies because of you, too. To my illustrator Pooja Jadav: thank you for making the concepts in this book sing with your delicious illustrations and visualizations.

Thank you to Carlos Andujar, Anthony Armendariz, Natalie Armendariz, Clasonda Armstrong-Grandison, Sarah Azpeitia, Ernestine Walls Benedict, Elizabeth Benker, Dontae Benn, Sara Bray, Margot Bloomstein, Katie Boyd, Joshua Blankenship, Brian Blomer, Claudia Bonitatibus, Jennifer Brook, Amanda Buck, Travis Burkstrand, Lina Calin, Leslie Camacho, Mike Carbone, Travis Castillo, Tom Censani, Gina Charalambides, Stephanie Choi, Matt Christians, Giancarlo Cianelli, Josh Clark, Nick Cochra, Anthony Colangelo, Matt Cook, Scott Cook, Chris Coyier, Geof Crowl, Joe Dagandan, Jesse Dawson, Kevin Deal, Lauren Deal, Theresa Diederich, Mark Dorison, Oliver Dumoulin, Patrice Embry, Harold Emsheimer, Jacob Esparza, Caroline Fay, Hilary Fenton, Abby Fretz, Vitaly Friedman, Brad Frost, Ian Frost, Katie Furstoss, Athena Gardner, McKenna Green, Corey Greeneltch, Mel Gross, Rob Hadley, Erika Hall, James Hall, Jessi Hall,

Kate Halvorsen, Tricia Han, Brent Hardinge, Jason Head, Gayla Hilton, Nam Ho, Vince Holleran, Dave Homa, Hayley Hughes, Mark Huot, Jon Jackson, Gina Villavicencio Joelson, Tim Kadlec, Joe Karasek, Beth Kettelkamp, Billy Kiely, Hunter Kievet, Jonny Klemmer, Wolf Klinker, Jamie Kosoy, George Kurtas, Jon Larama, Aidan Legaspi, Ahava Leibtag, Veronica Lin, April Lucero, Josh Luciano, Lisa Maria Martin, Adam McClean, Nina Mehta, Ryan Miller, Mary Mulvey, Rob Nashed, Octavius A. Newman, Teddy Ni, Erin Nicolle, Chris O'Brien, Rob Parisi, Jared Payne, Anthony Pino, TJ Pitre, Katie Potochney, Aziz Ramos, Hethal Rathod, Jen Reiher, Joe Rinaldi, LaRia Rogers, Darian Rosebrook, Isaac Ruiz, Dave Rupert, Greg Sarault, Madeleine Sava, Caroline Scheinfeld, Warren Schultheis, Tony Sciantarelli, Jaime Sena, Nadine Serraj, Tim Shelburne, Jan Six, Afyia Smith, Woo Song, Sara Soueidan, Isabel Sousa, Ken Sparks, Jonathan Stark, Anton Sten, Noah Stokes, Eric Thompson, Ben Turk Tolub, Eric Ulken, Dylan Valade, Mary van Ogtrop, Crystal Vitelli, Neil Vogel, Matt Walker, Mary Warrington, Mikaila Weaver, Kristopher Widholm, Jeremy Won, and Amanda Wunderley. The insights in this book came directly from my work with you. I don't take that privilege lightly.

Thank you to the giants of design systems whom I've learned leagues from and whose shoulders I stand on: Jina Anne, Mike Aparicio, Mathieu Badimon, Danny Banks, Joey Banks, Andy Bell, Maya Benari, Linzi Berry, Demian Borba, Garth Braithwaite, Ben Callahan, Mae Capozzi, Andrew Couldwell, Nathan Curtis, Anna Debenham, Kaelig Deloumeau-Prigent, Natalie Downe, Sarah Drasner, Dan Eden, Yasmine Evjen, Derek Featherstone, Sarah Federman, Jules Forrest, Jacqui Frey, Kathryn Gonzalez, Maya Hampton, Kelly Harrop, Henri Helvetica, Amy Hupe, Kyle Hyams, Aayush Iyer, Charlotte Jackson, Isha Kasliwal, Joanna Kirtley, Alla Kholmatova, Daryl Koopersmith, Inayaili de León, Lauren LoPrete, Eddie Lou, Tatiana Mac, Rune Madsen, Michael Mangialardi, Ethan Marcotte, Aylin Marie, Jono Mallanyk, Mina Markham, Sean McIntyre, Karen McGrane, Donella Meadows, Diana Mounter, Adekunle Oduye, Heather Palmer, Yesenia Perez-Cruz, Heydon Pickering, Stephanie Rewis, Michael Riddering, Natalya Shelburne, Alex Skougarevskaya, Matt D. Smith, Stephanie Stimac, Roy Stanfield, Marco Suarez, Miriam Suzanne, Katie Sylor-Miller, Donna Vitan, Trent Walton, Kim Williams, Jennie Yip, and so many more.

 Rosenfeld®

Dear Reader,

Thanks very much for purchasing this book. There's a story behind it and every product we create at Rosenfeld Media.

Since the early 1990s, I've been a User Experience consultant, conference presenter, workshop instructor, and author. (I'm probably best-known for having cowritten *Information Architecture for the Web and Beyond*.) In each of these roles, I've been frustrated by the missed opportunities to apply UX principles and practices.

I started Rosenfeld Media in 2005 with the goal of publishing books whose design and development showed that a publisher could practice what it preached. Since then, we've expanded into producing industry-leading conferences and workshops. In all cases, UX has helped us create better, more successful products—just as you would expect. From employing user research to drive the design of our books and conference programs, to working closely with our conference speakers on their talks, to caring deeply about customer service, we practice what we preach every day.

Please visit ⋒ **rosenfeldmedia.com** to learn more about our **conferences**, **workshops**, **free communities**, and **other great resources** that we've made for you. And send your ideas, suggestions, and concerns my way: louis@rosenfeldmedia.com

I'd love to hear from you, and I hope you enjoy the book!

Lou Rosenfeld,
Publisher

RECENT TITLES FROM ROSENFELD MEDIA

Get a great discount on a Rosenfeld Media book:
visit **rfld.me/deal** to learn more.

SELECTED TITLES FROM ROSENFELD MEDIA

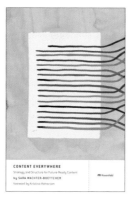

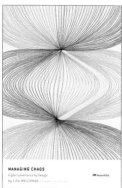

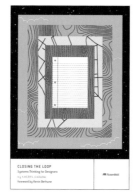

View our full catalog at **rosenfeldmedia.com/books**

 **Dan Mall** is a husband, dad, teacher, creative director, designer, founder, and entrepreneur from Philly. He runs Design System University, where he creates, collects, and curates curriculum, content, and community to help enterprise teams design at scale. Previously, Dan ran a design system consultancy, SuperFriendly, for over a decade. Dan writes about design systems, process, leadership, and other issues on his site **danmall.com** in his weekly newsletter. When he's not hanging out with family and friends or designing, Dan spends time shooting landscape photography, collecting sneakers, and playing basketball poorly once or twice a week.